A Hertfordshire
Christmas

A Hertfordshire Christmas

Compiled by
Margaret Ashby

The
History
Press

Frontispiece: Hitchin under a blanket of snow. Photograph by Ken Tipping.

First published 2005
Reprinted 2006, 2013

The History Press
The Mill, Brimscombe Port,
Stroud, Gloucestershire, GL5 2QG
www.thehistorypress.co.uk

British Library Cataloguing in Publication Data.
A catalogue record for this book is available from the British Library.

ISBN 978 0 7524 3679 1

Typesetting and origination by Tempus Publishing Limited
Printed in Great Britain

Contents

Acknowledgements

I acknowledge with gratitude the help of writers, publishers and agents who allowed copyright material to be included in this edition of *A Hertfordshire Christmas*. Full details are given with each extract. I have tried very hard to trace all copyright owners and to give appropriate acknowledgement. If, inadvertently, I have omitted anyone, please accept my sincere apologies.

Many other people have also helped and I would like to express my thanks to them, especially: Ken Woodruff for the drawings; Ken Tipping and Peter Jones, for their photographs; the Revd Don Dowling for writing an article specifically for this book; the families of the late Molly White and the late Revd John King; Ian and Patricia Aspinall, Judith Faraday, Archivist to the John Lewis Partnership, Clare Fleck, Archivist at Knebworth House; Betty Game; Joan Hale; Hertfordshire Archive & Local Studies staff; Steven Hodges; Gillian Robertson; Robin Harcourt Williams, Librarian and Archivist of Hatfield House.

Other books by Margaret Ashby:
Book of the River Lea
Book of Stevenage
Forster Country
Stevenage History & Guide
Stevenage Past
Stevenage Streets
Stevenage Voices
Voices of Benslow Music Trust

Introduction

It has given me great pleasure to compile a second edition of the anthology *A Hertfordshire Christmas*. I have been able to retain many of the items from the first edition and add some new extracts and illustrations. Researching and collecting the material has been most enjoyable as I have made contact with so many interesting and helpful people from all parts of the county. Perhaps because it is so near London, Hertfordshire has very few specifically local customs, but several writers have studied the county's traditions and extracts from their work are included in the anthology, along with an article on the origin of Father Christmas himself. There are descriptions of a wide variety of Christmas celebrations, from those of a Russian Grand Duke at Knebworth to paupers in the workhouse at Hitchin, from the long gallery at Hatfield House to soup kitchens at Berkhamsted, from shopping at Watford to carol-singing at Ware – and many more. To many of us, Christmas without music is unthinkable and here Hertfordshire does have something special to offer in the carols of a Hertfordshire composer and authority on Christmas music. Christmas is a time for storytelling and *A Hertfordshire Christmas* includes extracts from the work of some of the many eminent novelists who have been associated with the county, such as Jane Austen, Anthony Trollope and Charles Dickens. Modern novels, short stories and poems are also represented, their subjects ranging from seasonal reflections to ghostly tales. The tone of many extracts is inevitably nostalgic, as writers recall childhood Christmases, but it is also realistic. Probably none of us has ever experienced a perfect Christmas. Poverty, illness, cruelty, loneliness, disappointment;

all these stand between the idealised image and actuality. Yet, paradoxically, some of the most memorable and beautiful Christmas celebrations described took place in the least propitious situations – a TB hospital and a prisoner-of-war camp. With all its imperfections, its much-criticised commercialism, its muddle of the religious and the secular, the spiritual and the grossly corporeal, Christmas remains the outstanding festival of the year. It is the one time when families and friends everywhere make a particular effort to get in touch, renew their bonds of affection and create an atmosphere of goodwill. Statistics may show that Christmas is also a time for divorce, family rows and bitterness, but these things do not negate the joy of happy children, the laughter of friends gathered together, the exultation of Christmas music. Not everyone has the same vision of Christmas but it is to be hoped that, whatever our Christmas experiences, at least one was so happy that its memory stays with us as a warm glow to comfort and inspire the future. Hertfordshire Christmases, despite their lack of distinctive customs, are very special to those of us who love this understated county. I hope that *A Hertfordshire Christmas* will give as much enjoyment to those who read it as it did to me in compiling it.

Margaret Ashby
2005

A Christmas Donkey

Every year, donkeys from the Sandon Stud take part in Christmas services in churches at Sandon, Therfield or other North Hertfordshire villages. Owner Gillian Robertson leads the donkey in, helped by a small boy dressed as Joseph, with a tiny Virgin Mary on the donkey's back and a troop of angels following behind. The photograph shows Anna Law with Sandon Serafina, in Therfield church.

December
by Hope Bagenal

Hope Bagenal was an architect by profession and this poem, written at his home, Leaside, Hertingfordbury, was first published in the journal of the Architectural Association. Subsequently it appeared in a collection of his poetry entitled Sonnets in War and Peace *published by Oxford University Press in 1940. It is reprinted by permission of his son, John Bagenal.*

Winter through mild December still delays;
Nor yet beneath a snowy coverlid
Hath laid the earth asleep and green things hid;
But warmth prolongs these peaceful days and days.
The robins leave the berries on the sprays,
Eyeing the lawn by tender earthworm thrid;
And bulbs push up their mouths naught to forbid;
And on the wall the winter jasmine stays.

Merciful season bringing Christmas in –
The lantern sun hangs in the coppice trees:
It sinks and happy children troop within,
And Christmas windows waken by degrees:
From hearths of men ladders of smoke arise,
Reaching unshaken to the entranced skies.

Leaside, 1931

The Night Before Christmas
by Lois Clark

Lois Clark was a professional ballet dancer before her marriage. Although she appeared fragile, her dance training gave her the strength to work as a stretcher-bearer during the London Blitz in the Second World War. Her poetry often dealt with these adventurous and dangerous times. She lived near the abbey in St Albans until her death in 1988. A prize-winning poet, some of whose work has been heard on the BBC, Lois Clark was for many years a member of the Ver Poets, to whose editor, May Badman, I am indebted for this information, since it has proved impossible to trace her relatives.

Our world lies
lost beneath an infinity of stars;
a clarity, a beauty
we do not deserve;
fields gleam in their pale wash of light
innocent as lambs, and trees
wear white lace, frost-fingered.

Silence
holds this night in close embrace;
the night hoards her secret
as a woman hides
bright eyes behind a fall of hair;
only the swinging steeples
hum.

'The Night before Christmas'.
Drawing by Ken Woodruff.

No need
to search these skies for a guiding star,
they are all here tonight,
so bright the brilliance is a promise,
an invitation;
another dimension there, world beyond worlds,
a luminosity
in which anything is possible.

Christmas
In Medieval Hertfordshire
by Diana Norman

Diana Norman's novel, Fitzempress' Law, *published by Hodder & Stoughton in 1980, begins in the twentieth century with a motorbike accident, then transports its characters back to the twelfth century when Henry II (Henry Fitzempress) ruled England. Set in and around Datchworth (Tachwerte) the novel evokes life in medieval Hertfordshire in all its harshness and beauty.*

On Christmas Eve the convent church was transformed into a part of the countryside. Holly, yew, laurel, ivy and bay covered its walls, making it more of a sacred clearing in the forest than a stone church, part of the frozen landscape where hares made tracks in the snow and an owl swooped under a cold moon. Its only light was moonlight coming through the high windows and a single candle which stood on the altar.

The nuns fixed their eyes on the candle as they knelt and trembled, not from cold but from the mystery of their religion. For them Mary existed now. They saw her at this minute in labour, sweating, her body contracting. Outside in their Hertfordshire landscape an angel was addressing some frightened shepherds, and a long way further off, but travelling hard, the Magi had started out.

The prioress' hunched figure in front of the altar straightened and flung up its arms, palms curved upwards, holding a wet, invisible, little body. 'He is born.'

Swiftly she took the candle and lit others standing ready. The nuns joined her, rushing round the church lighting torches. Some of them laughed, some of them wiped away tears and laughed. Douceline and her sister jumped up and down. In blazing light and warmth, they swept into the nearest thing to a pagan song the Christian Church countenanced, Adam's Christmas hymn:

> *Frondis floris, nucis, roris.*
> *Pietate Salvatoris*
> *Congruunt mysteria.*

The mysteries of leafage, flower, nut, dew, are the Saviour's tender love.

> *Frons est Christus protegendo,*
> *Flos dulcore nux pascento,*
> *Ros coelesti gratia.*

Tatchwerte mourned the death of Aubrey until Christmas Day and then stopped, and gathered in Alward's hall for the Yule feast, determined to enjoy itself. It stuffed down marvellous luxuries like white bread, spiced beef and venison, honey cakes and mead like animals feeding up for hibernation.

They shrieked with laughter at the entertainers sent over by De Valogne to do some acrobatics and sing quite filthy ditties. They cheered the Yule log, they danced and played Blind Man's Buff, retired to be sick, returned to eat and laugh some more.

Len, knowing them, thought there was something frenetic in their revelry which came partly from the horror of the murder and partly from unease that they had not declared the murder to the sheriff's men.

They had refused to, despite urgings from Father Hervé and Alward. The Wild Hunt had done it and you couldn't convict fairy folk, they said. All that would happen would be that they would have to pay a fine for not producing a culprit – as had happened last time.

'And if you tell 'em Ulric,' Pusey had said, 'you'll be killed.' It was so obvious a statement of fact that Ulric had become frightened. He sat now with his wife, smiling eagerly as the rest played Fox and Chickens, as if he would like to join in but didn't dare. The village blamed him unremittingly for putting Aubrey in the way of her death by stopping her marriage.

Len might have felt sorry for him if he hadn't been too busy coping with Edeva who was drunk and was running around the room, cackling, turning her back on selected friends and hitching up her skirts to show her bare bottom. Now she was showing it to Alward but he, even though tipsy, remained a rock of common sense, slapped it and picked her up, wading through the chaos to plonk her down next to Len.

'Want to go and fart at Ulric,' she said amiably.

'Well you can't,' said Len. The noise was hurting his ears and the smoking Yule log made his eyes smart.

There was a sudden cold in the hall and the noise quietened down. In the doorway stood a tall young knight with the body of an old man in his arms. A confident, angry young man he was; the old man looked very ill.

'Come on you lot,' said the knight in a voice accustomed to command. 'I need help.'

It was Pete.

Davy's Christmas
by Gavin Daneski

✚

An RSPCA inspector based in south-west Hertfordshire, Gavin Daneski wrote about his experiences in The Animal Man, *published by Robert Hale in 1990. As this extract shows, he discovered that human beings, as well as animals, needed his help. Copyright Gavin Daneski, reprinted by permission of the estate of the late Gavin Daneski and A.M. Heath & Co. Ltd.*

Being so busy, time seemed to fly by, and before we knew it, Chris and I were making arrangements for Christmas.

Come the first cold snap of the winter, I was dragged from my warm bed by an early morning call from the fire brigade, requesting my attendance at a fire at Davy Crockett's caravan.

I arrived to be greeted by chaos, the like of which I had not seen before!

Davy was running frantically between a nearby stream and the blazing caravan, clutching a bucket. But, sadly, the bucket had more holes than bucket and was virtually empty by the time he returned to the inferno.

The dogs thought all this a grand game and chased Davy up and down enthusiastically.

'The silly old fool's turned up his stove too high again,' the fire chief told me. 'He did the same last winter.'

The firemen's efforts were being seriously hampered by one of Davy's dogs, who had a strong aversion to uniforms of all kind, as I

17

'Davy's Christmas'.
Drawing by Ken Woodruff.

knew from experience. Seeing the massed ranks of uniforms before him, he proceeded to take large lumps out of various trouser seats. This upped the already high temperature as distraught firemen leapt into the air before beating a hasty retreat back to the safety of their fire-engine.

'Don't just sit there. Do something!' Davy shouted, before making another futile run to the stream pursued by his canine helpers.

But by now it was a lost cause. The caravan's skeletal metal frame could be seen silhouetted against the dawn skyline. Davy finally admitted defeat.

'What are you going to do now?' I asked him.

'I'll have to see if Mr Harris can help me again,' he said, going on to tell me of a local benefactor who had originally bought the charred remains that now confronted us.

For the time being, though, his dogs had one of their regular

Ponies in snow at Norton Green, 1979. Photograph by Peter Jones.

holidays at Southridge, which they always seemed to enjoy, while Davy sorted out his latest disaster.

Two weeks later, on Christmas Eve, I received a telephone call – reverse charge, naturally – from Davy. Apparently Mr Harris had found another caravan for him, so he was ready to have the dogs back for Christmas.

To go with his smart new caravan, we found Davy looking equally restored from his ordeal, kitted out with purchases from the local Oxfam shop, his ever-present war medal pinned proudly to his smart new coat. To ensure that the new outfit received a proper christening, on being reunited with Davy the dogs bowled him over in traditional manner to celebrate the occasion.

'Happy Christmas, Davy,' I said, handing him a parcel.

'I haven't got you one,' he replied, wrestling excitedly with the wrapping-paper.

'The best present you can give me is to promise that you'll use it,' I replied, showing him how to operate the modern camping stove I had bought him, fitted with an inbuilt extinguisher in case of accident.

'That'll do a treat. Thanks, boy,' he said, suggesting we have a brew-up to master the new apparatus.

''Ow's the little 'un?' Davy asked, as we sat in his smart new home. I bet she's a little cracker.'

'You'll see for yourself tomorrow,' I told him, having arranged for Davy to have lunch with us, warning that he might not see much of me, as, being the 'new boy', I was having to cover most of North London for emergency calls, allowing my neighbouring colleagues to enjoy the festivities.

'Kids make it a real Christmas,' he mused, in rare philosophical mood. 'That's the one thing I really regret.'

'Not having children, you mean?'

'Yes.'

'I must admit they do make it a bit special,' I replied, glowing at the prospect of filling Charlotte's first stocking.

'But my dogs make up for it,' he said, watching them romp outside as we supped our tea.

'Oh well, I'd best get on, Davy ... I've a stack to do before Santa calls.'

'Make sure you check Rudolf tonight,' he laughed. 'I'm sure he gets overworked Christmas Eve.'

'I will,' I smiled. 'See you tomorrow ... Happy Christmas.'

'Happy Christmas, boy,' he replied, waving me off.

Decorating the Church
by Florence L. Barclay

Florence L. Barclay lived at Hertford Heath, where her husband was vicar, for thirty-nine years from 1881. During that time, as well as taking a lead in village life and bringing up a large family, she wrote ten novels which attained immense popularity throughout the world. This extract is from The Following of the Star *and is dedicated to 'my son in the ministry'.*

This last Sunday of his ministry at Brambledene chanced to fall on Christmas Eve. Also, for once, it was true Christmas weather.

As David walked to church that morning, every branch and twig, every ivy leaf and holly berry, sparkled in the sunshine; the frosty lanes were white and hard, and paved with countless glittering diamonds. An indescribable exhilaration was in the air. Limbs felt light and supple; movement was a pleasure. Church bells, near and far away, pealed joyously. The Christmas spirit was already here.

'Unto us a Child is born, unto us a Son is given,' quoted David, as he swung along the lanes. It was five years since he had had a Christmas in England. Mentally he contrasted this keen frosty brightness, with the mosquito-haunted swamps of the African jungle. This unaccustomed sense of health and vigour brought, by force of contrast, a remembrance of the deathly lassitude and weakness which accompany the malarial fever. But, instantly true to the certainty of his high and holy calling, his soul leapt up crying: 'Unto *them* a Child is born! Unto *them* a Son is given! And how shall they believe in Him

'Decorating the church'. Drawing by Ken Woodruff.

of whom they have not heard? And how shall they hear without a preacher?'

The little church, on that morning, was bright with holly and heavy with evergreens. The united efforts of the Smith and Jones families had, during the week, made hundreds of yards of wreathing. On Saturday, all available young men came to help; Miss Pike, whose taste was so excellent, to advise; the school-mistress, a noisy person with more energy than tact, to argue with Miss Pike, and to side with Smiths and Joneses alternately, when any controversial point was under discussion.

So a gay party carried the long evergreen wreaths from the parish-room to the church, where already were collected baskets of holly and ivy, yards of scarlet flannel and white cotton-wool; an abundance of tin-tacks and hammers; and last, but not least, the Christmas scrolls and banners, which were annually produced from their place of dusty concealment behind the organ; and of which Mrs Smith remarked, each year, that they were 'every bit as good as new, if you put 'em up in a fresh place'.

During the whole of Saturday afternoon and evening the decorative process had been carried on with so much energy, that when David came out from the vestry on Sunday morning he found himself in a scene which was decidedly what the old women from the alms-houses called 'Christmassy'.

His surplice rasped against the holly-leaves, as he made his way into the reading-desk. The homely face of the old gilt clock on the gallery facing him, was wreathed in yew and holly, and the wreath had slipped slightly on one side, giving the sober old clock an unwontedly rakish appearance, which belied its steady and measured 'tick-tick'. Also into the bottom of this wreath, beneath which the whole congregation had to pass in and out, Tom Brigg, the doctor's son, a handsome fellow and noted wag, had surreptitiously inserted a piece of mistletoe. This prank of Tom's known to all the younger members of the congregation, caused so much nudging and whispering and amused glancing at the inebrious-looking clock, that David produced his own watch, wondering if there were any mistake in the hour.

Christmas at Noningsbury
by Anthony Trollope

✠

Trollope lived at Waltham House, Waltham Cross from 1859 to 1870, during which time he wrote a number of novels, including Orley Farm *(1862) from which this extract is taken. At Christmas, he and his family played games such as those described here.*

The children, and there were three or four assembled there besides those belonging to Mrs Arbuthnot, were by no means inclined to agree with Mr Graham's strictures as to the amusements of Christmas day. To them it appeared that they could not hurry fast enough into the vortex of its dissipations. The dinner was a serious consideration, especially with reference to certain illuminated mince-pies which were the crowning glory of that banquet; but time for these was almost begrudged in order that the fast [*sic*] handkerchief might be tied over the eyes of the first blindman.

'And now we'll go into the schoolroom,' said Marian Arbuthnot, jumping up and leading the way. 'Come along, Mr Felix,' and Felix Graham followed her.

Madeline had declared that Felix Graham should be blinded first, and such was his doom. 'Now mind you catch me, Mr Felix; pray do,' said Marian, when she had got him seated in a corner of the room. She was a beautiful fair little thing, with long, soft curls, and lips red as a rose, and large, bright blue eyes, all soft and happy and laughing, loving the friends of her childhood with passionate love, and fully expecting an equal devotion from them. It is of such children that our wives and sweethearts should be made.

'But how am I to find you when my eyes are blinded?'

'Oh, you can feel, you know. You can put your hat on the top of my head. I mustn't speak, you know; but I'm sure I shall laugh; and then you must guess that it's Marian.' That was her idea of playing blindman's buff according to the strict rigour of the game.

'And you'll give me a big kiss?' said Felix.

'Yes, when we've done playing,' she promised with great seriousness.

And then a huge white silk handkerchief, as big as a small sail, was brought down from grandpapa's dressing-room, so that nobody should see the least bit 'in the world', as Marian had observed with great energy; and the work of blinding was commenced. 'I ain't big enough to reach round,' said Marian, who had made an effort, but in vain. 'You do it, Aunt Mad,' and she tendered the handkerchief to Miss Staveley, who, however, did not appear very eager to undertake the task.

'I'll be the executioner,' said grandmamma, 'the more especially as I shall not take any other share in the ceremony. This shall be the chair of doom. Come here, Mr Graham, and submit yourself to me.' And so the first victim was blinded. 'Mind you remember,' said Marian, whispering into his ear as he was led away. 'Green spirits and white; blue spirits and gray −,' and then he was twirled round in the room and left to commence his search as he best might.

One of the rules of blindman's buff at Noningsbury was this, that it should not be played by candlelight, − a rule that is in every way judicious, as thereby an end is secured for that which might otherwise be unending. And therefore when it became so dark in the schoolroom that there was not much difference between the blind man and the others, the handkerchief was smuggled away, and the game was at an end.

'And now for snap-dragon,' said Marian.

'Exactly as you predicted, Mr Graham,' said Madeline: 'blindman's buff at a quarter past three, and snap-dragon at five.'

'I revoke every word that I uttered, for I was never more amused in my life.'

'And you will be prepared to endure the wine and sweet cake when they come.'

'Prepared to endure anything, and go through everything. We shall be allowed candles now, I suppose.'

'Oh, no, by no means. Snap-dragon by candlelight! Who ever heard of such a thing? It would wash all the dragon out of it, and leave nothing but the snap. It is a necessity of the game that it should be played in the dark, – or rather by its own lurid light.'

'Oh, there is a lurid light; is there?'

'You shall see;' and then she turned away to make her preparations.

To the game of snap-dragon, as played at Noningsbury, a ghost was always necessary, and aunt Madeline had played the ghost ever since she had been an aunt, and there had been any necessity for such a part. But in previous years the spectators had been fewer in number and more closely connected with the family. 'I think we must drop the ghost on this occasion,' she said, coming up to her brother.

'You'll disgust them all dreadfully if you do,' said he. 'The young Sebrights have come specially to see the ghost.'

'Well, you can do ghost for them.'

Victorian engraving of worshippers arriving for a Christmas service.

'I! No; I can't act a ghost. Miss Furnival, you'd make a lovely ghost.'

'I shall be most happy to be useful,' said Sophia.

'Oh, Aunt Mad, you must be the ghost,' said Marian, following her.

'You foolish little thing, you; we are going to have a beautiful ghost – a divine ghost,' said uncle Gus.

'But we want Madeline to be the ghost,' said a big Miss Sebright, ten or eleven years old.

'She's always ghost,' said Marian.

'To be sure; it will be much better,' said Miss Furnival. 'I only offered my poor services hoping to be useful. No Banquo that ever lived could leave a worse ghost behind him than I should prove.'

It ended in there being two ghosts. It had become quite impossible to rob Miss Furnival of her promised part, and Madeline could not refuse to solve the difficulty in this way without making more of the matter than it deserved. The idea of two ghosts was delightful to the children, more especially as it entailed two large dishes full of raisins, and two blue fires blazing up from burnt brandy. So the girls went out, not without proffered assistance from the gentlemen, and after a painfully long interval of some fifteen or twenty minutes, – for Miss Furnival's back hair would not come down and adjust itself into ghostlike lengths with as much readiness as that of her friend – they returned bearing the dishes before them on large trays. In each of them the spirit was lighted as they entered the schoolroom door, and thus, as they walked in, they were illuminated by the dark-blue flames which they carried.

Unforgettable Yuletides
by James Birdsall

James Birdsall and his two brothers were brought by their parents to live at Walkern during the Second World War. These recollections of Christmas at The Cottage are taken from his book The Boys and the Butterflies. *Copyright James Birdsall, 1988. Reproduced by permission of Chrysalis Books Group Plc.*

The earlier wartime Christmases were very special. Nowadays Christmas and New Year punctuate the season before the long wait for spring, but one knows it will all be round again next year. Then we couldn't be so certain. A year is a long time when it represents some fifteen per cent of Life so Far, and there was the constant underlying fear that the war and family life and indeed Christmas itself could be lost before the next one had worked its way through. This very doubt made the festival a precious one and the friendly, 'all-in-it-together' atmosphere, so prevalent during the days of trial, was heightened at Christmas time.

Getting ready for Christmas started fairly early in that greetings had to be sent abroad to friends and relations in the services and those of the family still in India. These would take the form of airgraph letters. The original draft was on an official form rather larger than quarto size on which you wrote your letter and did your drawing, for no letter was complete without a drawing and with any luck you could get away with considerably more drawing than correspondence. Tim carried this into later life. At the height of his short career as illustrator and cartoonist, he would write to me with a letterhead of gigantic size with some four lines of 'good, newsy letter' underneath. Our airgraphs would be photographed down to a small negative, flown out along with thousands of others, and enlarged the other end. Those coming to us in reply would be about five inches high and you had to read them with a magnifying glass.

We would get mysterious parcels which had to be hidden until Christmas. Tins of exotic sweets would come from Aunt Marjorie, Dad's sister in the Queen Alexandra's who as a nursing officer followed the Eighth Army across the African desert, into Sicily, up through Italy and then crossed into Normandy in the wake of the liberating armies, finishing up in Germany itself. In 1945 King George decorated her with the Royal Red Cross, First Class. The sweet tins were sewn into canvas and stamped and censored and altogether looked as exciting as the contents. One, filled with Turkish Delight, arrived years late, battered out of shape, the ship having been sunk to the bottom of the Red Sea and the cargo later retrieved. The sweets were quite undamaged by their ordeal.

There were parties at our village school, and the inevitable village concert party to which we all walked, carrying our gas masks, with opaque blue paper pasted over our torches so that we could just see to tread safely without alerting enemy aircraft. Old friends and old protagonists in unfamiliar guises, singing popular songs, performing sketches and cracking jokes which we hardly understood but laughed loud with everybody else. 'Something About a Soldier' and 'When They Sound the Last All-Clear' and 'There'll Always Be an England!' But mostly Christmas was a family affair at home. The Cottage lent itself to Yuletide decoration like the traditional Christmas card

The White Lion, Walkern. Drawing by Ken Woodruff.

with a robin in one corner and church bells in the other. The bells, of course, were silent throughout the land as they were reserved as an alarm in the event of the invasion. The ropes in the church tower were hoisted high out of reach where they hung in an intriguing parabola with their gaily coloured woolly lagging visible over the carved oak screen at the back of the aisle. Mr Bayes the butcher had given us a treasure chest of old, pre-war tinsel and trimmings to which we added our own laboriously made paper streamers and Chinese lanterns. Precious baubles and tree lights were handled with care and unwrapped from orange papers and later packed away again cautiously, for who knew when one would be able to buy such things again? The predominating motif was of holly, ivy and mistletoe

31

culled from the trees and hedges and nailed on to the interlacing oak beams as though they had grown there all the year round. A huge oak Yule log burned for days on the dogs in the inglenook, surrounded by smaller satellites of hornbeam which, when the bark was off, were delicately fluted like Edinburgh Rock. We felt a glow from the products of our labours in the woods which was not entirely due to the sparks and the blaze.

We had a house full for the Christmas of 1942 – there were Mum's brothers, Uncle Arthur, who had got his wings, and Uncle John, who was a Desert Rat, and a New Zealander friend of his with an enormous moustache like a shoe brush, known simply as 'Whit'. By the next Christmas all three were dead. I often reflect with something of a shock that I am the longest surviving male scion of the Edwards family for many generations. They were all killed in wars. My maternal grandfather, a doctor, was killed in 1917 when my mother was only ten. He never saw Arthur, his youngest. My grandmother, she of the black hair and blue eyes, died shortly afterwards, it was said of a broken heart. Arthur's eldest daughter was there at The Cottage as a baby that Christmas. He in his turn never met his youngest.

A festivity which started in the war years and became quite an institution in the village was our New Year's Eve fancy dress party where we toasted the New Year in at nine o'clock in cider. Children would start asking Mum about it around September and would their little brother be old enough to come this year? In the first one Tim made a stunning Bo-Peep with crinoline and petticoats devised from pre-war evening dresses long out of service and cardboard bonnet and ribboned crook. 'Uncle' Len, always ready with an apposite

Woodland snow scene. Photograph by M. Ashby.

quote from the 'Halls', sang, 'Coom, pretty one, coom, coom, coom, coom!', whereupon the disgruntled shepherdess pulled the customary faces and flounced off to get dressed as a pirate. Dr Stein was always recruited as a convincing Father Christmas and the Rector would look in, wearing an impossible false beard and fool nobody. Around eight o'clock would come an urgent telephone call for Dad and he would hastily disappear in the car while 'Uncle' Len's womenfolk, 'Aunty' Beet and 'Aunty' Ethel, would cluck in sympathy for the poor Doctor whose time was never his own. I later found out the emergency took the form of a vacant hand at crib at the White Lion – I had wondered about the regularity with which patients would take a turn for the worse during the annual fancy dress party.

Charades were an essential part of the entertainment and we cheated shamelessly. 'Granulated' came up once, as in sugar. How the syllables were enacted, I forget, but the final word was represented by a gruesome emergency appendectomy in the family kitchen: 'Gran, you lay Ted on the table and I'll sharpen the bread knife!' When everybody had gone and we were ready for bed, we were allowed down to the inglenook, for Ghost Stories and Pictures-in-the-Fire.

Rosehips in winter. Photograph by M. Ashby.

One of the Family
by John Stroud

John Stroud began his distinguished career with Hertfordshire County Council in 1952, as a Child Care Officer. In his first novel, The Shorn Lamb, *he wrote about boys such as Lenny, who was due to leave school at Christmas but had nowhere to live. In desperation his Care Officer considered boarding him with an elderly couple who had a spare room. Copyright John Stroud, 1960. Reprinted by permission of the author and A.M. Heath & Co. Ltd.*

We went to see the bedroom the boy would have: I wasn't too pleased with it, it was rather dark, bare, and neglected. But by this time I'd made up my mind that this was worth a try for Lenny, these people wouldn't lightly give up a job they had once undertaken. We arranged that Lenny should come to them for the Christmas holiday, and that if there was no startling incompatibility he should stay on with them and get a job.

'I think you'll find him a nice quiet lad,' I said, as I was leaving. 'So long as you don't rush him.'

'Lor' bless yer, sir,' said the old lady, slapping her thigh, 'can yer see us folk rushin' anybody?'

Westburn seemed more than usually loud and vulgar when I got back to it that night.

I wrote to the people whom the Parchments had given as referees and all the answers said much the same thing, that these were excellent old people, but didn't I think perhaps they were a bit too old. By this time, however, the memory of Lenny's imploring eyes had made me decide that he must go to Much Furbish as arranged and I took him over there the week before Christmas. He was very quiet on the way. A burnt child fears the fire.

But as soon as we got in the door, Mrs Parchment said: 'Hallo, lad, come and get your tea,' and she produced from the old-fashioned oven a vast steak and kidney pudding and set it before him and then sat by the fire with her hands folded in her lap and twinkled at him.

'Come up an' see 'is room, sir,' said Mr Parchment, in a hoarse whisper. When I got up there I paused in the door-way, staggered by the transformation. The room had been newly decorated with a pink rosebud wallpaper and bright white paint and there were new curtains and shining lino on the floor.

'We thought we'd like to 'ave it proper for 'im,' said the old man.

Goodness, I thought humbly, all this has been done out of the old-age pension.

I didn't see Lenny again for a while as we were terribly busy with Christmas, but I sent him a card with icicles on it, and a postal order, and went up again in January. He wasn't in when I arrived, but the old folk told me that he was getting on alright with his job, he was rather slow and he didn't always grasp an instruction the first time, but once he knew what he had to do, he went right on with the job till it was finished.

'And how is he with you at home?' I asked.

There was a long silence and then they both screwed up their eyes, nodded and said together:

'All roight.'

'One of the family'. Drawing by Ken Woodruff.

And Mrs Parchment added: 'Seems loike 'e's bin 'ere all 'is loife.'

There was the sound of loud whistling outside and a bike was cheerfully clattered about, and in came the lad himself.

'Ah, Mum! Dad! Sir!'

I hardly recognised him. He was bigger and heftier and ruddier and happier. We didn't have much to say that evening, I sat and beamed and nodded and Lenny glowed at me over his enormous supper, and what talk there was was largely monosyllabic. The old folk sat and regarded him with that peaceable loving pride that a carpenter shows for a long tried tool. I began to recognise in myself that bitter-sweet feeling that I was an intruder, that they wondered why I bothered to come. Lenny had dropped anchor.

In the middle of February I got a telephone call from someone I didn't recognise.

'This is Mrs Bean speaking,' she said. 'Mrs Bean from Much Furbish.'

Ah, yes, of course, this was Rosie, Mrs Parchment's daughter.

'Good morning, good morning!' I hailed her.

'Sir, I'm sorry to bother you, I thought you should know, sir,' she said. 'My mother died last night.'

'I-I-I'm so sorry, I'll come at once,' I said, and as I put down the telephone, I could feel the blood ebbing from my hands and feet.

I got out to the cottage as fast as I could, and Rose took me through to the back room. The old man was sitting in the front room, reading his Bible. He bowed to me gravely as I went past.

'I'm terribly sorry about this,' I said to Rose. 'I feel as though I have lost a friend.'

'It must come to all of us,' said Rose.

'I can take Lenny back with me now if you wish,' I said. 'I'd like to try and find a home in the village for him, but of course you won't want him here at the moment.'

'Why, sir, you don't mean to say you're taking him away? Our Lenny?'

'Well, I – surely you – I assumed –'

'Sir, my husband and I will move in here to look after Dad and Lenny. But of course we shall, sir. Lenny is one of the family now.'

The Puckeridge Hounds

✚

The Puckeridge Hounds, established in the early eighteenth century, took their name from the hamlet of Puckeridge, which is situated at the junction of the A120 and the Old North Road (A10). In 1970 they merged with the neighbouring Newmarket & Thurlow Hunt. This letter from 'Black Coat', originally published in a newspaper, has been quoted in a number of books on foxhunting, but the identity of the author remains unknown.

Sir, – These hounds had one of the best hunting runs I ever saw, in this or any other county, on Friday 24th. The meet being Throcking, the Springs was first drawn, but no fox at home this time; the next draw was Mr. Wilkin's covert, Broadfield, which generally holds a good fox, although he is not a hunting man himself. The hounds were no sooner in covert than Ned, the whip, viewed a fox over the ride, but there appeared to be no scent, as hounds could not speak to it. The fox broke covert on the Friars side, but being headed, went back through the covert, and out by the farm, away to Awney, the hounds hunting him nicely over the grass. When they got through the covert on the plough, the Cottered side, many thought it was all over; Hedges held the hounds on down to the road, close to Sir W. Call's training-ground. Not being able to hit it off, he made his cast to the right, for Cumberlow Green, and soon had them on his line again, going over the Cromer road, leaving Cumberlow on his right, up to within one field of Cold Ash covert, onto the old Roman-road, which he ran up to the cottage on the hill, when he

Edwardian hunting scene, artist unknown.

turned to the right, going between the Howell Springs, no doubt
thinking of going to ground in the dell, where a litter of cubs was
bred last spring; but when we got there a lad was stopping the earths,
and some thought he was stopping the fox in, but the hounds soon
told us he had gone on over the open for Box Wood, but being
headed, he bore to the left down to Walkern Village, through the
cottage gardens, over the Stevenage road, bearing to the right, as
though he meant working his way round to Box Wood; but altering
his mind went to the left, to a little covert at Aston End. This was
the first covert he touched after leaving Awney, which is from seven

to eight miles as the crow flies. He then went away for Bennington High Wood, but when he got to the brook in the bottom, he ran by the side of it until he came to the Bennington and Aston road, then crossed over, pointing for Lowfield Grove, turned to the right, and went back over the brook and on to Astonbury Wood, where he beat us. No doubt he went to ground, as the earths were all open, although hounds could not mark him. Time up to Astonbury Wood, one hour twenty-three minutes. I was sorry the Squire was not out to see his pack hunt their fox in the way they did. Hedges told me he had not been out since he heard of the death of his old friend, Mr Foljambe.

'Black Coat'
December 24th, 1869

Haunted Abbey
by Betty Puttick

✠

This true story is from Betty Puttick's Ghosts of Hertfordshire, *published by Countryside Books. Reprinted by permission of the author and Countryside Books.*

It was a crisp, cold Christmas Eve as a 16-year-old youth made his way up the hill towards the great Norman Abbey, standing serene in the moonlight, dominating the city of St Albans as it had for hundreds of years.

On this special night of the year people should have been flocking there for the Christmas Midnight Mass as the bells pealed out the age-old summons to celebrate the birth of Christ. But the Abbey was dark and silent, the twelve huge bells removed from the belfry, for it was 1944, England was at war, and the young man who let himself in through a side door was there as one of a team of fire-watchers. It was their job to spend the night in the Abbey in case of fire bombs, and to make a regular check of the whole building and the fire-fighting equipment. Nights like this, with what people called a 'bomber's moon', required extra vigilance.

There was no sound but his own echoing footsteps on the stone-flagged floor as Basil Saville made his way through the vast dark shadowy building to the vestry. He walked confidently for, as he had been a chorister, the Abbey was a familiar place to him, but when he discovered that no other fire-watcher had arrived, he had to admit that the thought of guarding this historic edifice on his own was a daunting prospect.

But it had to be done, so when no one else came, he set off on the regular tour of the building. It was cold and frosty outside, but the Abbey seemed even colder, with that deep penetrating chill of old churches, and the moonlight filtering faintly through the windows made the shadows even deeper.

Basil felt uneasy, something wasn't quite as it should be, and he tried to shrug off a growing feeling that although his regulation hooded torch revealed nothing untoward, he was not alone in that ancient holy place.

He followed his usual route through the Abbey, checking the water containers, stirrup pumps and hoses as he went, until he reached the Saint's Chapel where the Shrine of Saint Alban stands, and an early fifteenth century watching chamber from which monks used to keep a vigilant eye on pilgrims visiting the martyr's shrine.

The feeling that he too was being watched was very strong now, and as Basil shone his torch high up into the watching chamber he felt the hairs on the back of his neck rise as he thought he could glimpse two hooded figures. He called out, then climbed the rickety old staircase up to the loft, but his torch revealed no intruders and he knew no one could have passed him. His heart beat faster as he noticed two monks' habits lying there on the floor, but Basil tried to reassure himself that they must have been used for some theatrical production, although he could not recall anything of the kind.

He was relieved to reach the blacked out Lady Chapel where at last it was possible to switch on some light, and he sat for a while trying to collect his thoughts, conscious of the lonely emptiness around him, then continued his patrol.

On his way to the twisting staircase which led to the roof he almost fell against one of the Abbey's twelve great bells which had been stored on the ground floor for the duration of the war. But as he climbed into the upper regions above the nave he all but lost his balance as suddenly a bell began to toll in the belfry. How could this be happening? Hadn't he nearly tripped over one of the bells down below? And yet the steady tolling went on, so summoning his courage he opened the belfry door as the sound died away and found, as he knew he would, that there were no bells hanging there.

The tolling had stopped and, confused and at a loss to understand his extraordinary experiences, Basil climbed out on to the roof of the tower, standing there in the moonlight, grateful for the cold fresh air on his face.

But the events of that strange Christmas night were not yet over. As he started back down the stairs, the organ began to play and looking towards the organ loft he saw a candle flickering by the console but could not see the organist. Instinctively he called out the fire-watcher's familiar warning – 'Put that light out' – and moved to get a better view.

There was no one seated at the organ and yet, from his vantage point above, Basil could see the pages of a book of music turning, and the organ keys being depressed by unseen fingers. Then suddenly from the direction of the high altar came a glorious burst of singing.

Hardly knowing what he was doing, Basil hurried down the stairs and through the Abbey towards the choir stalls. The music had stopped now, but as he looked towards the high altar he saw a magnificent sight. A procession of monks with their abbot, all holding candles, were leaving the high altar and passing through

The Roman wall of *Verulamium*, St Albans, *c.* 1970. Photograph by M. Ashby.

the screen doors into the Saint's Chapel. The doors closed behind them, and Basil followed to the chapel, only to find it empty and in darkness. He ran back and climbed up to the organ loft and, in the light of his torch, found a spent candle and a book of music. Here at least was some tangible evidence that he had not imagined the whole extraordinary experience.

The book was quite large, with plain black covers and yellowing manuscript pages. Opening it he read the title, *Albanus Mass* by Robert Fayrfax.

Back in the vestry, he was relieved to find his fellow fire-watcher had arrived. The other man had apparently heard and seen nothing, and together they went round the Abbey again, as Basil told his companion about the strange events he had witnessed. But when they reached the organ loft the used candle he had seen was no longer there, and the two monks' habits had disappeared from the floor of the watching loft.

Had it all been a dream? But after all these years the powerful impression of that wartime Christmas Eve remains with him.

'I was stunned by it – overwhelmed,' he recently told me. 'I'm not psychic or anything like that,' he added, 'and I've never seen anything like it either before or since. People may not believe me, but I know it happened.'

St Albans Abbey. Drawing by Ken Woodruff.

Christmas Memories
by Graham Greene

Born and brought up in Berkhamsted, the eminent novelist Graham Greene described his childhood Christmases in A Sort of Life, *the first volume of his autobiography. Extract from* A Sort of Life *by Graham Greene, published by Bodley Head in* 1971, *reprinted by permission of David Higham Associates.*

At the far end of Berkhamsted at the Hall, the great house of the town, lived the family of Greene cousins. The mother was German and the whole family had an intimidatingly exotic air, for many of them had been born in Brazil near Santos, on a *fazenda* which was also the name of the coffee we drank. There were six children, the same number as in our family, and in ages they were inserted between us, our family starting first, as though my uncle, who was the younger brother, had suffered from a competitive spirit and wanted to catch my father up. My own particular friend was Tooter, though it was with his younger sister Barbara that I was years later to make the rather foolhardy journey through Liberia which I have described in *Journey Without Maps*.

My uncle's children were the rich Greenes and we were regarded as the intellectual Greenes. We would visit them on Christmas Eve for the Christmas tree, my elder siblings staying for dinner. I used to be embarrassed by the carols in German round the tree because I was afraid I might be expected to sing too. The whole affair in our eyes seemed rather Teutonic, for to us the eve of Christmas had no significance at all. Christmas only began the next morning with the crunchy feel of a heavy stocking lying across the toes and a slight feeling of nausea, due to excitement, which bore the family name of a 'Narcissus tummy-ache'. I don't remember any Christmas tree in our house, and mistletoe was an embarrassing joke played by our elders. Kissing had no appeal, and I kept well away from the mistletoe if anyone else were around.

On Christmas Eve, at the Hall, the children all had their presents laid on separate tables which were identified by names on cards. I remember being bitterly disappointed once when an adult present, a leather writing-case, on my table, turned out to be there in error: it was intended for my uncle, who bore the same name and who was the Permanent Secretary of the Admiralty and a Knight of the Bath – a title which I found impressive and not funny at all.

Memories of Bernard Shaw at Christmas Time

by Allan Chappelow

George Bernard Shaw lived at Shaw's Corner, Ayot St Lawrence from 1906 until his death in 1950. Fellow residents of the village later contributed their memories of the great playwright to Shaw the Villager and Human Being: a biographical symposium, *narrated and edited by Allan Chappelow and published in 1961 by Charles Skelton Ltd. The following three extracts are reprinted with permission from Allan Chappelow.*

Miss Jisbella Lyth, legendary village postmistress of Ayot St Lawrence remembers –

That reminds me of an amusing story about Miss Patch, Mr Shaw's secretary at Whitehall Court. She came to Ayot sometimes, but only on rare occasions when her work necessitated it. Once she was here at Christmas time – it must have been around 1943. At breakfast she complained to Mr Shaw, 'It's not a bit like Christmas. I never *was* in a house where there was less of the spirit of Christmas. I'll have to write that down in my diary.' 'Oh!' said Mr Shaw, with that twinkle in his eye, 'I didn't know you kept a diary!'

Shaw was never much affected by birthdays and Christmas and so on. The old adage is, of course, that genius and madness are akin, but that hardly applies to Shaw. He was an exception to the rule – there was nothing mad about him – a bit eccentric and cantankerous at times, perhaps. He was exceptional in that he was so great that he was able to combine his artistic nature, his genius if you like, with being an ordinary man as well – at least, that's how I found him. Some would say, I suppose, that it was eccentric of him to order all his stamps from me by letter, but I prefer to regard it as simple kindness. I've sold almost all those letters now, of course – I believe he meant them to be a sort of legacy to me. I'll never forget how he used to joke about it and say I'd only get 2½d each for them – but, as I've told you, I've been getting up to three guineas apiece!

Memories of James Thomas Williams, a fellow villager of Ayot –

He always took an interest in anything that went on in the church and came when John Hunt gave a recital on the organ, and when the Sunday School children presented a Nativity Play. He thought the play was well acted and produced, but his criticism was that one of the Kings should have been black. I remember once when we met him on our way home from school. He had recently returned from a visit to South Africa, and said: 'It's fantastic how the black people dance to hymns. I think people in Europe should dance to hymns as the black people do. It's a pity that in England they are so solemn about their religion. They should sing, "O, You Must Be a Lover of the Lord, or You Won't Go to Heaven" in church, and dance to it.'

When the Sunday School went carol-singing outside his house he contributed generously, as he did for anything connected with the children of the village. But he would not address at that time the Women's Institute, though begged to by my mother-in-law. He says in a letter to her about this (written from Ireland 1923), 'I never speak now in public, even on politics, when I can help it; and as to speaking

Ayot St Lawrence post office.
Drawing by Ken Woodruff.

on Art, Literature, Music, Drama, Humane Killing, Vivisection, and all the other subjects in which I am supposed to be eloquent, I should spend the shortened remainder of my life on the platform without a single evening's respite if I hesitated to reply a brutal "No" at every petitioner.'

Harry S. Rayner, the postman who, for many of Shaw's most active years, delivered and collected his letters, remembers –

In the blackout – in 1940 or thereabouts – I was the postman who made the final collection at Ayot, at 6.00 p.m. On one occasion I got there at about 5.57 p.m. I picked up some parcels and registered letters from Mrs Lyth, and then cleared the box. But I was very surprised to find that there were none of Mr Shaw's letters and postcards there. I thought he must have had an off day. I checked the time. It was one minute to six. I locked up the box, and by the time I had done this and was ready to move off it was two minutes after six. Then Mr Shaw rolled up. 'You've cleared the box early,' he charged me, and we had quite an argument about it. He had his Norfolk jacket on and pulled out his watch from his pocket. I said that I had checked my watch an hour before at the post office and it was 'spot on', and told him he should buy himself a new watch. 'Well, I *never!*' he exclaimed. The next day he apologised and said I was quite right – his watch *had* been slow by the radio later that evening. He took it very good-humouredly. That was the only time I ever remember him being late for the post.

I was in the War Reserve and did service for most of the Second World War. I was back at work at the post office by Christmas 1945, doing my old round. Mrs Laden told me that Mr Shaw wanted to see me. I went into him. He shook hands and asked me where I'd been and what I'd done, and said, 'Are you coming to deliver and collect my letters again? I've missed you.'

A few days later he gave me £3 Christmas Box in an envelope addressed: 'To my Postman with the Compliments of the Season.' I was surprised at his generosity as I'd only been back a fortnight.

Garden snow scene. Photograph by M. Ashby.

The Christmas Pastimes, 1894

from Memories of Canon Woolmore Wigram by his wife,
published by Swan Sonnenschein & Co. Ltd in 1908.

The Revd Woolmore Wigram was vicar of Furneaux Pelham from 1864 to
1876 and rector of St Andrew with St Nicholas and St Mary, Hertford from
1877 to 1897.

These were held in the first week of January, for the fourth year in
St Nicholas' Hall, and for the seventh time since they were first really
organized. They were as usual very charming, and the young actors
have improved wonderfully in clearness of speech, in pronunciation,
and in the power of acting. Some of the scenes, especially the drilling
of the Amazon army, were very pretty. It would be impossible to
carry out these performances without the kind, voluntary, and skilful
help of the relations and friends of the children; and we feel that
particular thanks are due to Mrs Wigginton, Miss Mary Ilott, Miss
Beddall and Miss A.M. Wigram. Besides the interest and amusement
the Pastimes gave during the dull, dark days of this winter, they were
of substantial benefit to the Hall Fund, realizing £8 10s towards the
Mortgage Debt, and giving 16s to the Piano Fund.

It may interest our readers to have a list of the plays acted since
1890:-

The Sleeping Beauty
Rumpelstiltskin

Jack and the Beanstalk
Cinderella
Snowflake and the Seven Gnomes
Beauty and the Beast
The strayed Falcon
Aladdin
The Twelve Dancing Princesses
Ali Baba and the Forty Thieves
The White Cat
Puss in Boots
The King of the Black Isles
Hop o' my Thumb
The Invisible Prince

In 1894 an attempt was made at a
different kind of entertainment –
tableaux vivants illustrating Church
History. That of St Dorothea was
first chosen. Woolmore gave the
readings, and hymns were sung
between the scenes; no applause was
allowed, and the whole was performed very reverently and beautifully.
Another time the history of St Agnes was given in the same manner.
Lectures were arranged from time to time – one cannot really
enumerate all the various means used to keep the parish alive – not
only to amuse but to elevate, interest, and teach them.

A Village Christmas
by C.M. Spicer

Mary Spicer combined careful historical research with memories of her childhood in Shephall to create Tyme out of Mind. *Chapter 12 includes recollections of Christmas at the village school. Extract reprinted from* Tyme out of Mind, *published in 1984 by C.M. Spicer and D.M. de Salis, by permission of the author.*

About the time I started at the village school, when I was five, Mrs Tresidder arrived, the new head teacher. She devoted herself to the village, becoming Sunday school teacher, church organist and choir mistress. She was a widow with two children; a keen botanist, she would frequently take a crowd of children out on Saturdays for nature walks and picnics. We had a nature table at school filled with dozens of paste pots, each with specimen flowers, or with seeds in the autumn. They each had a card with the Latin name of the plant and its order as well as the more familiar name. Each child also kept a nature diary. In retrospect I can see she was very up to date with all her teaching methods.

The large schoolroom held most of us, the small classroom being rather cold and dismal, and at that time there were seldom more than two dozen children between the ages of five and eleven. The infants were taught by a pupil teacher. In the winter there was an open coal fire, and a large iron stove in one corner; both were well protected by guards which in winter frequently had coats, socks and other items

The patriotic finale of the 1930 Shephall School concert. Mary Spicer is holding the portrait of King George V.

put to dry, some of the children having to walk a mile or more. The windows were high and all that could be seen were birds and trees, although we could hear the horses and carts coming and going at the farm next door. In the summer the room was light and airy with doors and windows open. Outside were two separate playgrounds for boys and girls, although in practice we often played together – the boys' playground behind the school was overhung by trees and damp. Each had their own earth closet, and in the girls' playground was a wash-house with an enamel bowl for washing hands, and a pump which creaked and groaned before ejecting rusty water.

The school day started with worship and before and after we went home to dinner we sang graces. Not all the children could get home; some brought sandwiches, or had aunties or grandparents near. We had a sports day during the summer but the big event of the year

The church at Aston, neighbouring village to Shephall.

was the school concert. After the summer holidays we began learning songs, recitations and a play. As Christmas drew nearer, handicraft lessons were given over to making paper garlands and to making and mending tinsel wands or fairy wings – because there were always fairies! The boys had jackets and trousers of old sheets, one year trimmed with pom-poms as pierrot clowns, trimmed up some other way the next year, and later the whole lot into a tub of green dye to turn the boys into elves! There was always a patriotic song to finish, with much red, white and blue bunting and flag-waving. On the day a stage filled a quarter of the big room, with smart black and white curtains dropping as background, and handsome brocade stage curtains. Seating was provided by every home sending well-dusted chairs (with names chalked underneath). The more comfortable chairs were at the front for the party from the Bury. When the Bevan family were living there the adult sons introduced some rather more syncopated rhythm from the London shows in an item or two! One year the children did a very lively offering of 'The Bells are Ringing For Me and My Girl!' for Mr Johnny and his bride-to-be, with a tiny bride and bridegroom, and arches of half-hoops embellished with paper roses. The bride was played by a very fair little boy, there being no little girl of the right size. At the end the bouquet was presented by a very bashful little bridegroom to the real life bride.

After the great day of the school concert and Christmas itself we could still look forward to the School treat. This was a tea with paste sandwiches, buns, cakes and jellies for all the village children. There was a huge decorated Christmas tree cut from the Bury grounds, and a visit from two elderly Heathcote ladies then living in Stevenage. Each child had a poke of sweets, an apple and an orange to take home. After tea we played games like Blind Man's Buff, Poor Pussy, Spinning the Trencher, Hunt the Thimble and Oranges and Lemons; danced a rather bashful Sir Roger de Coverley and perhaps had a magic lantern show.

December Seventeen
by Joyce Conyngham Green

✚

Joyce Conyngham Green's Salmagundi: being a catalogue of sundry matters *refers to many parts of Hertfordshire. Published in 1947, it was partly written during the Second World War, as this extract makes clear. Reprinted from* Salmagundi *by Joyce Conyngham Green, published in 1947 by J.M. Dent. Attempts at tracing the copyright holder have been unsuccessful.*

The December miniature from the book of hours shows the preparations for Christmas in the beginning stages. A table with a thick chopping-board top is set outside the back premises of a grey stone house, where a man-cook in a peach-coloured shirt, dandelion-yellow jerkin, ultramarine stockings, and a white apron is attacking a pig's carcass with a large cleaver and a businesslike manner, throwing each joint as he cuts it off – Shylock-wise, without one drop of blood – into a large two-handled basket. His assistant, clad in a lettuce-green shirt, cobalt jerkin, red stockings, and a white apron, is nervously singeing the bristles off a second animal, standing well away from it, with his knees bent and an air of expecting a general conflagration at any moment.

Over the yard wall can be seen a cluster of thatched, gabled houses, white, blue-grey, and a soft pinkish-yellow, which might easily be a Hertfordshire village such as Bramfield, Thomas à Becket's first living, with a 'rolling English road' winding among the cottages. Hertfordshire 'hedgehogs' seem to have believed from time immemorial that the longest way round is the shortest way home, or perhaps the plethora of inns in every town and village has something to do with the curling lanes.

As I looked at the pigs in the small picture my thoughts turned back to pre-war Christmases, and it had a rather damping mock-turtle effect on my mind. 'Once I was a real turtle', or rather, 'Once we had a real Christmas' with, apparently, peace on earth and goodwill towards men. The first sentence of this paragraph is too ambiguous; it sounds as if I connected pigs with Christmas dinner, human pigs, but actually my mind leapt from pigs to the 'hotel in Suffolk Street' so often mentioned by Trollope, where we spent several happy Christmases in the thirties, and where one of the items of Christmas lunch was always a sucking-pig; 'a dear pigmy'.

Then the other Christmases at my grandparents' house; how glad I am that they were able to keep up good solid Victorian middle-class habits into Georgian times, so that I can remember real family festivities with grandparents, great-uncles and aunts, uncles and aunts, cousins, friends, and, now almost as extinct as the dodo, smiling maids in crisp white aprons who entered ungrudgingly into the spirit of the season with as much gusto as the guests. What a mounting atmosphere of excitement prevailed on Christmas Eve as the great bunches of scarlet-berried holly were brought in to decorate the tops of the portraits in the dining-room and the pictures in the hall, while ears were kept on the stretch for the sound of the front doorbell and the chatter of voices which proclaimed further arrivals to swell the gathering.

How impossible it was to go to sleep with all the flittings and whisperings along the landings, and the stealthy openings and closings of doors. But somehow sleep did come at last, only to vanish in the small hours of the morning, when a sixth sense told the sleeper that it was time to grope for the bulging stocking 'all bubukles, whelks, and knobs' which had appeared mysteriously in the night-watches and now hung dropsically from the bed-knob. Though it was still dark and switching on the lights at unearthly hours was strictly forbidden under threats of unmentionable punishments, the stocking had to be pulled into bed, while questing fingers ran up and down its bumps with the intensity of concentration given by a phrenologist to an interesting subject. Half the joy would have flown if the small parcels had been pulled out and unwrapped at once – no, then it was a year between Christmases, not a few short weeks as now – and a stocking was a treasure to be gloated over in a miserly fashion. Each rustle from its interior as it was pinched and prodded was greeted by a stealthy chuckle. Stealthy, lest Nemesis should descend and whisk the precious object back to the foot of the bed again to be looked at when a more seemly moment had arrived.

No more presents were allowed until after breakfast. My grandparents disapproved of paper and string becoming tangled up with such serious pursuits as eating and drinking. I chafed under this prohibition then, but I see they were quite right now; I would give all the presents that I have ever had for half a dozen wafer-thin slices from one of their breakfast hams, delicately pink with a faint, translucent reflection of the colour running into the pearly fat with its edging of crisp, brown crumbs. The very memory of it makes me drool like a spaniel; but in those days I merely fidgeted because the grown-ups pottered so over their bacon and kidneys, their boiled eggs, their ham, their toast and marmalade, and their second or third cups of tea or coffee, little recking of the piles of thrilling parcels waiting in another room.

Bramfield post office. Drawing by Ken Woodruff.

How can I bear to think of Christmas dinner? At least twenty-six people always sat down at the long table with its snowy damask cloth, its gleaming silver, and glistening cut-glass. Mostly family and married-intos, with a friend or two for good measure, with all current hatchets which might be (metaphorically) flying about buried for the day in shallow well-marked graves, to be dug up and refurbished when the Christmas spirit had evaporated for another year. This, of course, is my grown-up mind putting two and two together of then unheeded, but none the less registered, incidents and remarks together and making them four. Still, what could be expected when two generations, eight brothers and six sisters-in-law in one alone, are contained in the company. The third generation present was mercifully too young for feuds.

The turkey matched the gathering in size:

> It was a Turkey! He could never have stood upon his legs, that bird.
> He would have snapped 'em short off in a minute, like sticks of
> sealing-wax.

Its skin held the soft glow of brown amber, its flesh the deep cream of old ivory, and oh! the savoury, relishing smell of the greenish-beige stuffing; to say nothing of the chestnut-brown of the accompanying sausages, for we always had 'an Alderman in Chains', to use the old name for a turkey so garnished. Epicures say that eight- to ten-pound turkeys are the best, but I never have tasted one to equal those served at my grandparents' table. And the pudding, as light in texture as it was dark in colour and admirably embellished by delicious pale gold brandy sauce; the mince-pies with their fragile pastry which fell into crisp flakes as the fork touched it, and their wine-flavoured fruity filling. Finally dessert: oranges, apples, pears, great purple grapes with a velvet-silver bloom – no, I cannot bear the recollection, I will turn to other memories.

The indefinable smell of the hall when the front door was opened, compounded of the scent of good cigars and lavender furniture cream in equal parts. The pearly grin of the old-fashioned papier mâché nigger-boy holding out a card-tray; the handsome bead-and-bamboo curtain which veiled the alcove where the umbrellas, the sticks, and the telephone lived, and which clashed so satisfyingly to and fro. Firelight glowing and flickering in a book-lined room, where my grandfather with his pointed silver beard and beautiful hands talked wittily of cabbages and kings, and where my grandmother with her bright blue eyes, creamy skin, and crown of hair which had turned blond, and not grey, with age, kept his more Elizabethan sallies under gentle but stern control.

Great white chrysanthemums and green trails of smilax forming the inevitable centre-piece to the Christmas dinner-table; one year the smilax crop had failed, a catastrophe equal in magnitude to holding the coronation with half the regalia missing. Jokes, phrases, and quotations, jargon to an outsider, often with their origins completely forgotten even by the initiated, but still perfectly intelligible in the family circle. The solemn ceremony of looking down every cracker before it was pulled in an endeavour to guess the contents, which was faithfully carried out by every one from the oldest to the youngest. Batgers' Chinese figs – Elvas plums – almonds and raisins...

Looking back, half the joy of those family gatherings was the unchanging ritual of the day; the certainty that each Christmas would be an exact replica of the last, as far as was humanly possible – a feature that is immeasurably more poignant now, when so many people have learnt what it is to live for years under the shadow of sudden death or mutilation – though I admit that this facet of the celebrations has only come to me while I have been writing of them. The sense of stability, of security, though both these things are but illusions at the best of times, so frail is the tightrope that we walk between happiness and sorrow.

A Composer's Christmas
by Margaret Ashby

The composer Elizabeth Poston lived for most of her life at Rooks Nest House, formerly the home of E.M. Forster and the inspiration for his novel Howards End. *The surrounding countryside is now known as the Forster Country. Reprinted from* Forster Country, *published in 1991 by Flaunden Press.*

Christmas was always a particularly strenuous time for Elizabeth. Both her carols, and she herself, were in demand for concerts locally and nationally. 'Jesus Christ the Apple Tree', which she wrote in her teens, had captured many hearts and was becoming one of the most frequently performed carols. She was always delighted when young people appreciated her music. One association which gave her particular pleasure concerned the Ward Freman School at Buntingford, of which she was to write later; '...a remarkable place I have long been interested in – they have adopted me and I them – charming, enterprising folk artistically go-ahead... Their two patrons have been me and Henry Moore and they are very sad at his loss. He was very kind to them and let them have marvellous exhibitions of his work from his home at Little Hadham. A year or two ago they built on the Poston Room, (complete with photograph!) for their music wing, and it has always been a very happy relationship. I don't like Christmas to go by without a visit...'

She tried to remember all her friends at Christmas,

Elizabeth Poston with her cairn terrier, Comfort. Photograph by M. Ashby.

Rooks Nest in snow. Photograph by M. Ashby.

especially old or frail people whose friendship went back to the time when Stevenage was 'the village'. Little pots of Rooks Nest honey or jam would be wrapped carefully in a piece of last year's Christmas paper and decorated with a sprig of winter jasmine, an ivy leaf or a stem of balsam, to which was added an affectionate message in her distinctive handwriting on the tiniest possible tag. How many of these reminders of Elizabeth are still preserved in the Forster Country or beyond? Many friends collected their presents when they came to Rooks Nest with their own gifts for her, but by Christmas Eve there were always a few packages remaining. Elizabeth, with Comfort beside her, would drive out into the night, to old Alfie's

Holly decoration at Rooks Nest. Photograph by M. Ashby.

cottage on the way to Weston; then on to Chesfield, where her headlights might illuminate the white plumage of a hunting barn-owl. A little parcel would be left at artist May Bloom's caravan at Crow End; yet another at the council flat in Stevenage where lived old Mrs Adams who once worked for her mother; then on again, until the round was completed, and the loving message of Christmas handed on for another year.

The Origins of Christmas Day

by Israel Worsley

✚

Little is known about Israel Worsley except that he was born in Hertford and was probably related to the Samuel Worsley who was pastor at Cheshunt Congregational Chapel in the second half of the eighteenth century. His An Enquiry into the origins of Christmas Day: shewing that this and other festivals of the Christian Church are continuations of the Heathen Feasts of antiquity, *from which the following piece is taken, was published at Plymouth in* 1820.

The Carols formerly sung at this season were not as they are now where they are continued, religious songs bearing an allusion to the birth of Christ: they were songs, calculated to enliven the merriment of the festival, they were bacchanalian songs. The old music of the

God of wine was performed by bands of singers passing through the streets and about the country; and traces of this practice are yet to be found in Yorkshire, where women begin with the feast of St Martin, to make peregrinations about the neighbouring villages, carrying a little waxen image and singing. Children do the same in small companies in most towns, still retaining at least a part of the bacchanalia, and collecting their little treasure.

Christmas boxes, so common within our remembrance, were instituted by the popish priests, who said masses for any thing and every thing for which they could get paid; among other things for the debaucheries and vices which were in a manner licenced at Christmas. A box was put up called the Christmas box, into which all were encouraged to throw money; and in order that servants, and labourers, and the poor in general might be enabled to contribute, they were invited to solicit box-money; well knowing the old proverb: no pay – no paternoster. It may be doubted whether a better use is made of the Christmas boxes in protestant countries. They too commonly nourish the licentiousness of those who receive them, instead of that of the priests.

Amongst these facts, which refer themselves distinctly to the paganism of Greece and Rome, we also distinguish strong marks of the northern manners which prevailed at this feast. One of the peculiarities still observable is the serving up of the flesh of hogs as a standing dish. In the Veda are verses to this effect, 'The cook dresses the wild boar incessantly in his pot; the heroes are fed with the fat of this animal, which exceeds every thing in this world.' These Nations appear to have had little other consideration but to eat, to drink, and to fight. The women are introduced only to fill their cups. The wild boar furnishes the whole of this banquet. The flesh of this animal as also the hog, was formerly the favourite meat of all these nations. The ancient Francs were no less fond of it. The head of the boar assumed a distinguished rank at the table – and old chronicles of this Island tell us, that the boar's head soused was the first dish that was served up on Christmas day, that it was carried with great solemnity to the principal table, a carol being sung whilst it was serving up. This custom is still retained, we are told, at Queen's College, Oxford, at Christmas time.

We learn that the ancient Danes were great topers: and, to encourage the habit of tippling, when anyone had transgressed the customs of the court, he was punished, by being obliged to drink a bumper out of a large horn, kept for that purpose in the palace. Our modern bacchanals have not therefore the merit of this invention.

Another custom which came from the northern nations into the British manner of celebrating Christmas, was placing upon this feast a branch of the Mistletoe on the altar; which, we are told was done in York Cathedral for many centuries after the establishment of Christianity. The ancient Druids held the Mistletoe in the highest veneration. Because it grew upon the Oak, and derived its nourishment from this king of the Forest, which was dedicated to their God Thor, as it was to Jupiter by the Greeks, it was regarded as an emblem of human dependance upon Deity, and they were accustomed to place at his feast the Mistletoe on the altar of that God. The early Christians thought to honour their Saviour-God by continuing to dedicate the Mistletoe to him on this day; it has been also stuck up in the windows; and on the mantle-pieces among the evergreens at Christmas.

In the primitive Church after the Heathen worship had given place to it in the north, Christmas day was always preceded by an eve or vigil. When the devotion was completed, our forefathers used to light up candles of an uncommon size, and lay a log of wood on the fire, which they called the Yule-log. A kind of baby or little image, intended to represent Jesus, and called the Yule-dough, was made up at this season, and presented by the bakers to their customers. – The Yule-log is still presented by journeymen carpenters in the northern counties to their master's customers, as a plea for a Christmas box – and we have also ourselves seen the Yule-dough.

In the sacrifices which were offered by the Egyptians to the Moon, upon which occasion the more wealthy presented swine, those persons who were indigent made the figure of one with meal, and having roasted it, offered this as their sacrifice. Hence the origin of the Yule-dough, as an emblem of the sacrifice of Christ; which might be afterwards very conveniently substituted by the Hot-cross-buns.

Christmas in
Victorian Times

By 'Beorcham'

Percy Birtchnell ('Beorcham') contributed regularly to the Berkhamsted Review between 1940 and 1960. The extract below is taken from an article which first appeared in Vol. 95, No. 12 and is reprinted here by kind permission of the chairman of Berkhamsted Local History Group.

Anyone who writes about Christmas in Victorian times has a bitter-sweet story to tell; the holiday was short, and so was money for a very large section of the community. But it was a poor heart that never rejoiced. As soon as one Christmas was over, cottagers started thinking of the next, joining coal and clothing clubs, usually run by a church or chapel, and paying a few coppers weekly or fortnightly for a little spending spree at Christmas.

Home-Made Toys

In early autumn, parents and children would start thinking about Christmas presents. From choice or necessity, most of those presents were home-made – clothes, for instance, and toys. Lucky indeed were the children of Berkhamsted's many woodworkers, whose dolls' houses and toy trains were often better than those sold in the shops.

Now we live in a do-it-yourself age, but how few of us ever *make* a Christmas present?

People with shillings to spare could afford luxuries which today cost pounds. But, pro rata, wages were much smaller than they are at the present day. A bottle of port could be bought for 1s 3d; rum, whisky and brandy cost 2s 3d a bottle, and at the grocer's one could buy a quart of champagne for 2s 1d. Pale ale, bought direct from a brewer, cost 1s 4d a gallon, and a Northchurch firm advertised tobacco at 4d an ounce. In 1893, David Pike sold pure honey at 6d a lb, and 40 Lisbon oranges for a shilling. In 1887, seven butchers had stalls in the market place; at the end of the day they were selling 10lb of beef for 3s. A novelty was 'highly perfumed Christmas and New Year cards', costing 1d to 5s.

Skating Galas

Christmas was always spent at home or with the grandparents. We always assumed that people enjoyed the entertainment they made themselves, and I hope that was true. For good measure a series of hard winters provided a very special pleasure that is known to few of the present generation – skating. Galas were held on the canal night after night, with fairy lamps twinkling and many a bonfire on the towpath to warm by-standers. St Peter's Band sometimes attended, and baked potatoes and hot coffee were supplied by William Fisher, who tempted providence by setting up a brazier on the ice. Collections were taken for unemployed men, who maintained good skating conditions by sweeping the ice.

Of course, most of the skaters made their way to and from the canal, or the Castle moats, on foot. Some of the fortunate few travelled by horse-drawn sleigh. I am indebted to Major Adrian Hadden-Paton for the information that in hard winters friends from miles around flocked to Rossway to skate on the moat, some of the parties arriving in sleighs, with bells jingling on the harness. Gregory, the butler, handed round claret cup and mulled wine to the skaters, a tricky job on the slippery banks of the moat.

That was over a century ago. Rossway was rebuilt in 1866, and in that year a charming tradition, continued for many years, was born. On Christmas morn, at 7 o'clock, the servants assembled in the hall and sang 'Christians, awake', to the strains of a concertina played by Gregory.

Drum And Fife Band

In the 1870s, the St Peter's Drum and Fife Band saluted the happy morn by playing a selection of music as they marched through the town between midnight and 1 a.m., varying the programme from time to time by stopping to sing carols.

One year the band spent Boxing Day at Cheddington, playing at farmhouses and dining in the village schoolroom off roast beef and plum pudding. The band returned by train and then 'enlivened the town for several hours'.

Next day, the drum and fife boys played at Northchurch 'and most of the surrounding genlemen's houses, where they met with a kind reception'. In the evening they went to The Hall, and played for nearly two hours before the High Sheriff, Capt. Constable Curtis, and his guests. The boys' band subsequently developed into St Peter's Town Band (now the Berkhamsted and Boxmoor Silver Band).

A Victorian mother and child.

Soup Kitchens

Hard winters brought unemployment, poverty and misery to dozens of families. Many a Christmas dinner would have been meatless but for the help given by district visitors and other charitable people. Free – or almost free – soup kitchens were installed at Foster's Brewery (behind the Swan) and in the Castle grounds. To quote the *Berkhamsted Times* of 1877:

> The soup distribution is an important event ... coming twice a week, Wednesday and Saturday, from eleven until about twelve o'clock, at the soup house in the Castle grounds. On Saturday last, some 340 families experienced the benefits of the excellent charity, which was accompanied by a distribution of bread (one pound to a pint of soup) from Balshaw's Charity.
>
> The recipients were admitted alphabetically, a policeman regulating their admission to the savoury precincts of the kitchen. Here two immense coppers were filled with the hot compound... On Saturday, the names were called out by Mr Alfred Miller, the treasurer, in conjunction with the Rector, who marked the book and stated that everyone on the list had attended. The treasurer received 17s in coppers at a farthing a pint, which shows that 816 pints were disbursed.
>
> From all parts of the parish came the people with their 340 tin cans, or other vessels, some of which, improvised for the occasion, were of an interesting description... A preserve jar, which a boy hugged in his arms, overflowed down his Saturday suit, though outside instead of inside, where it ought to have gone. Some of the boys were so hard pressed that on getting to a sunny side by the wall to the station, they used the lids of their cans for vessels and, pulling a piece off a loaf, had a roadside snack.

The busiest man in the town was the workhouse master; in 1887, 50 grown-ups and 21 children were in his care, and extra Christmas fare was provided for them. The number of people in receipt of out-relief was 488.

After Christmas there was a round of concerts, magic lantern shows and what were known as social teas. William Cooper, of the chemical works, entertained his staff to sumptuous feasts. There were glittering balls in the Town Hall. In turn, every large house held a lavish party, and the balls at Ashridge, Haresfoot, Rossway and other mansions were often dazzling affairs. That meant hard work for the servants, whose reward came with that once famous but now very rare event, the servants' ball, which sometimes lasted until it was time for the housemaids to start yet another daily round, cleaning the grates, whitening the hearthstones, filling the scuttles and starting roaring fires for yet another day of ease and comfort for the fortunate few.

Folk Customs of Christmas
by Doris Jones-Baker

Dr Doris Jones-Baker is the leading authority on Hertfordshire customs and folklore and has held many offices in the sphere of local history. In 1982 she was elected a Fellow of the Society of Antiquaries of London and, in 1984, Fellow of the Royal Society of Arts. The following extract is taken, with the author's permission, from her Folklore of Hertfordshire, *published in 1977 by Batsford.*

The folk customs of Christmas began, as did those of the church, with the coming of Advent. The four weeks which followed were the time when the wassailers (carol singers), the guisers (Mummers) and hand-bell ringers made the rounds of villages and towns performing as did the Waits in the streets, or by custom or prior arrangements for the upper classes, in the drawing rooms of vicarages and other homes of the well-to-do. In many places carol singers, now often led by the Vicar and making a collection for church or charity, still come round in much the same way, and in Whitwell and other places the parish bell-ringers with their hand-bells.

Carols in Hertfordshire have as long a history as in any County. The first English Carols to appear in print were included in the *Boke of St Albans*, said to have been compiled by Dame Juliana Berners, Prioress of Sopwell, and published by the 'Schoolmaster-printer' at St Albans in 1486. *Christmasse Carolles*, issued by William Caxton's apprentice and successor Wynkyn de Word, in 1521, is the oldest known printed book of English carols. Only one of its pages, the last containing the colophon, has survived, with two carols: 'A Caroll, bringing in the bore's head', and 'A carol of huntynge' – reprinted from the *Boke of St Albans*. One of the earliest surviving manuscript collections of carols, moreover, is in the early sixteenth century Commonplace Book of Richard Hill (Balliol MSS 354) of Hillend, Langley, in the parish of Hitchin, a member of the Grocers Company and Lord Mayor of London. More than half the 62 carols in Hill's Book relate to the Nativity, Epiphany, the Christmas Saints and the Annunciation.

No carol has yet been identified as of Hertfordshire origin, however, and it appears that Hertfordshire to some degree at least shared the carols of London and the Home Counties north of the Thames.

For singing at Christmas-tide, in the nineteenth if not in centuries before, was the winter counterpart to the 'Mayers Song' – referred to simply as 'The Old Christmas Song'. William Chappell in *Popular Music of Olden Time* (1855) identifies this as the tune for the traditional carol 'God Rest You, Merry Gentlemen', a version of which was printed as early as 1827 in *Facetiae* by William Hone. At the beginning of this century William Gerish in Hertfordshire noted that 'The Old Christmas Song' was sung in Sandon parish 'like the May Song' antiphonally, two lines at a time, with the entire company joining in the chorus.

In Hertfordshire – as in other places – there was a sharing of good and well-loved tunes among songs. About 1840 the Hoddesdon Waits used the following variant of 'The Old Christmas Song' tune as their setting for a 12-verse version of 'The Joys of Mary'. It was collected by the eminent folklorist Helen Creighton in Nova Scotia from Norma Smith of Halifax, who wrote of it:

> My grandfather [Saunders] used to sing this every Christmas Day until he passed on. He came to Canada from Hoddesdon, Herts. He would only sing this on Christmas Day, no matter how much we would coax to have it at other times. When he was a tiny boy the Waits used to sing it in the village, and when he was old enough he would steal away from home and sing it with them. He was born in 1833. Because of the demi-semiquavers at the end he said only an Englishman could sing it.

This tune, as sung by the Hoddesdon Waits about 1840, may have been the dominant version used – if not originated – in Hertfordshire. Most widely known today, however, is the so-called 'London' version (*Oxford Book of Carols*, 1928, No. 12) as printed by Dr E.F. Rimbault in *A Little Book of Christmas Carols* , in 1846. 'The Mayers Song', sometimes called after the beginning of one of the verses 'The Moon Shines Bright', was sung to 'The Old Christmas Song' at Christmas as well as around May Day. In Hertfordshire carol singers, bell-ringers, and other performers still follow the old tradition of performing their entire repertoire before appreciative audiences, regardless of the season.

A number of other carols have been associated with Hertfordshire. Among the earliest must be the secular songs of that master of medieval music and pioneer of new forms, John Dunstable (d.1453) who, it is thought may have been born in Hertfordshire and whose patron, the Duke of Bedford, was a brother of Humphrey Duke of Gloucester and a friend of John of Wheathampstead, Abbot

Christmas carol singers, 1881.

of St Albans, 1420-40 and 1452-65. Among the carols ascribed to Dunstable, who wrote the noted Motet for St Alban's Day, *Albanus roseo rutilat*, is 'Wonder Tidings', (*Oxford Book of Carols* , 1928, No. 40), which begins:

> What tidings bringest thou, messenger,
> Of Christes birth this jolly day?

A particular favourite in the nineteenth century was 'As I sat on a Sunny Bank'. Lucy Broadwood (d.1929) recorded an eight-verse version sung near King's Langley before the end of the century. Another version, with six verses that she heard as a child in Hertfordshire, is given by Elizabeth Poston in her *Penguin Book of Christmas Carols*, 1965.

In Hertfordshire, Christmas Eve was the popular time for the 'guisers', as the mummers were called, to make their rounds giving their traditional plays at the larger houses in the parish. It is to be regretted that no text or detailed description of a Hertfordshire mummers' play has been found. There is evidence, however, that Bishop's Stortford had a play about the legend of St Michael and the Dragon: St Michael was the patron saint, and the Churchwardens' Accounts mention both the 'pley' and the parish dragon, made of hoops with canvas stretched over them, who was not only a popular performer in the town but was rented out to Braughing and other neighbouring parishes for their plays as well. At Hexton plays about Robin Hood were given in Queen Elizabeth's reign, and probably later. The most curious survival of mumming, perhaps, is the graffito of a full-size Hobby Horse, deeply cut in the stone of the church porch at Wallington where the parish Hobby Horse was probably kept. The custom of 'guising' at Christmas is now no longer remembered: by the end of the nineteenth century the 'guisers' in the neighbourhood of Hitchin and Baldock performed only on Plough Monday in January.

Sweeping the snow, 1871.

Christmas at Ware in the 1830s
by James Smith

The writings of James Smith, who was educated at Ware Free Grammar School in the 1830s, have been edited, with an introduction, by David Perman and published under the title A Quaint Old-Fashioned Place *by Hertfordshire Publications, 1990. This extract presents a picture of his youthful Christmases.*

Christmas Eve brought in snapdragons, bowls of spiced ale called 'lambs' wool', mulled elderberry wine, and the carol singers. The childish voices of the latter, quivering with cold, narrated 'the seven good joys that Mary had', or described in doggerel verse how:

> As it fell out upon a day
> Rich Dives sickened and died,
> There came two serpents out of hell,
> His soul therein to guide.

At midnight the 'waits' came round, – survivors of the minstrel watchmen formerly attached to the royal court, whose duty it was to announce the passing hour in a short strain of music. And at such an hour, with a good band, composed of stringed and reed instruments, playing a selection from Mozart's 'Twelfth Mass', you could not help feeling the exquisite truth of two lines in *The Merchant of Venice*:

Portia – Methinks it sounds much sweeter than by day.
Nerissa – Silence bestows that virtue on it, madam.

It was among the pretty traditions of the period that, on Christmas Eve, the bees might be heard singing in their hives; the oxen might be seen kneeling in their stalls; and if you applied your ear to the ground, you would be sensible of the ringing of peals of subterranean bells.

Not to have gone to church on Christmas Day, of all the good days in the year, would have been an inexcusable social solecism, as well as a breach of a religious duty. The building was quite a spectacle. The pillars and arches, the galleries and chandeliers, the brass lectern and the carved pulpit, the antique font, and the very organ itself were masked with holly and ivy, bay, laurel, and other evergreens. The roomy old family pews, in which you could slumber so comfortably on hot drowsy Sunday afternoons in the summer time, were filled with troops of children home for the holidays. The 'gentry' from the Park were accompanied by other 'gentry' from London, whose costumes were the admiration and envy of the less fashionable townsfolk. The services were more musical than usual, and Luppino, the organist, used to regale our ears with a grand 'voluntary' which brought out all the powers of one of the finest instruments in provincial England. As to the sermon, it was short and sweet, genial and practical. There was the largest offertory of the year, and Meares, the Sexton, and Mrs Meares, the pew-opener, used to stand at the entrance of the great porch to receive their annual donation from the worshippers. Outside there were friendly greetings innumerable, family enquiries, invitations 'to come round in the evening', and an interchange of the compliments of the season. The keen frosty air seemed to be pervaded by an odour of roast turkey, and from the

'The mode in 1898: a pretty evening dress'.

bakehouses there soon streamed forth a procession of working-men's wives carrying home the steaming Christmas joint. The afternoon and evening were devoted to social enjoyment, prolonged far into the night; and next day, if the weather was favourable, every sheet of ice in the neighbourhood was populous with skaters. A succession of parties enlivened society until Twelfth Night, when the Christmas season virtually closed. Once, I remember a wealthy maltster, whose nephew is an enterprising citizen of Melbourne, gave a concert in the Town Hall at his own expense, and brought from London the finest vocal talent of the day. It was a munificent act of hospitality, and the invitations embraced nearly all classes of society.

Christmas at Clare Hall Hospital in Wartime
by Molly White

Although warned by her family that she was not strong enough to take up nursing, Molly White left her home in Newport, Monmouthshire at the age of nineteen to train at a London teaching hospital, where she worked among people in dire poverty. When the Second World War broke out she tried to enlist for the Queen Alexandra's Nursing Corps, but was turned down because she was not sufficiently robust. Instead, she spent the war as a ward sister at Clare Hall Hospital, on the borders of Hertfordshire and Middlesex.

Clare Hall was a specialist chest hospital. All the patients had TB and most of the staff. When people came out of the services with TB the authorities tried to put them into chest hospitals as near to their homes as possible, so most of our people came from north London. It was easier for visitors. In the earlier days there was no public transport so buses were put on to bring them on Sunday afternoons.

My ward was in the converted concert hall at first. The stage and curtains were still up. There was one lavatory and when you pulled the chain the roof nearly collapsed. The wards and operating theatre were being built and when they were finished my ward had two loos, but the patients were too ill to get up. I had 28 very ill patients from the London Chest Hospital.

89

Chest surgeons came from London, from the Royal Free and the Middlesex Hospitals. They used to go round the wards on Mondays, to see those waiting for surgery. These patients had been waiting a long time, some for two years.

We had no mod cons – just the building. There were black coke stoves in the middle of the room. The stoke hole was outside. I had to take patients to the theatre. All the operations were done under local anaesthetic because the patients were not strong enough for a general.

There was a big fish kettle in the corner and we had to boil all the surgical instruments in that, to sterilize them. We used to cut dressings and put them in a 7lb biscuit tin which was placed in a gas stove. Amazingly, we never had any cross-infection.

The patients became part of your family. Matron used to come round with her dog, on a social visit. She was one of the old school, very strict. We were never allowed cardigans, although the place was always half open and very cold. One day she asked, 'Why have the nurses all got holes cut in their shoes?' I said, 'They have all got chilblains.' I made an ointment for them with lard and mustard.

On one visit, Matron asked, 'Have you had tea?' I had not had time, as I had been dealing with operations all day. Matron said, 'Go to the kitchen and I will stop with the patients.' When I got back she said, 'There's nobody speaking English in this ward.' 'No,' I said. 'How do you manage?' asked Matron. 'Well, I have a dictionary and somehow we do manage. Also I put written instructions over each bed.'

Most of the staff were refugees or escapees from prison camps. There were Latvians, Poles, Germans. One Latvian had crossed the border in the boot of a car. I had a most wonderful Latvian girl. She was a trained pharmacist and spoke about six languages.

Molly White.

Newcomers always had to be medically examined, but it was difficult to get them to undress. Often they were wearing everything they possessed. The first thing they wanted was to go to evening classes, but there was nowhere to go. There were no buses, we were out in the sticks. We couldn't go anywhere. In any case they had to register with the police every week. But we used part of one of our buildings for lessons. Every morning they asked, 'Has the post come?' Some of their relatives were prisoners of war. They were all young.

We had to try to boost their spirits. I said, 'Now what about Christmas, girls, what shall we do?' We had a tin to save coppers in, and staff and patients saved a penny a week. Patients hadn't done any shopping for about two years, they didn't know you couldn't get hairclips etc.

I had always been keen on markets. It was five miles to St Albans and five to Barnet. I decided to cultivate St Albans market. I had never had a bicycle, but I received a bicycle allowance of £1 a month and I put this towards the Christmas treats. The market sold a lot of damaged goods. There were many Jews from the east end of London who came there with materials that had been bomb damaged. For instance, there were two men who got things from bombed buildings, such as tea spoons and cups with handles, or jars to put sugar in.

There was a nice little woman, oh she was lovely. I said, 'Have you any remnants to make bedjackets for Christmas?' She said, 'Would it matter if they didn't match?' 'Oh no,' I said. 'I work in a hospital and its very cold. The patients are cold after their operations.' One week the market lady said, 'See what you can do with these' and produced a bag full of quilting pieces from a factory.

Two ladies from the village offered to help. They made 'granny' shawls for when the patients sat up after their operations. At this stage they always had one arm they couldn't use, so shawls were ideal. We made bed jackets with Magyar sleeves from the pieces of quilting. There were enough for everyone, so that those who could not afford it were all the same.

Our resident chest surgeon was Mr Laird. When he took his wife to the pictures I had to ring up the cinema if there was an emergency and they would put a message on the screen for him. He and his wife were very kind. He suggested having a theme for the wards each Christmas. One year he said, 'Let's go to Holland at tulip time.' I thought this would be easy, so we cut out paper tulips and stuck them in the fireguard and made bonnets and caps out of paper. For the men's wards he suggested the theme of railway stations. Whichever ward got the most marks for its decorations won a prize and there was great excitement when the judging took place.

On Christmas Eve everyone had their hair in curlers and a stocking hanging on each bedpost. In the early evening the staff went from ward to ward singing carols and afterwards we finished dressing the tree.

Mr Laird always came with his children on Christmas Day. He would dress up with one of his wife's aprons and a bonnet. We always had a turkey by some miracle and once he said, 'I can't carve this!' I said, 'You do better with human beings.' The staff had a 'Christmas Dinner' of cold meat and rice, which they ate when they could snatch a few minutes away from the ward.

We listened to the church service on the wireless and after lunch a few visitors came, those who could manage transport. Then there was an hour's rest for the patients while the staff had a rather splendid tea with little treats that had been saved through the year with the help of kind friends in the villages.

In the evening the girls who couldn't go anywhere came to my ward in wheelchairs. My husband dressed up as a chef and served the meal of cheese and celery and a visitor played the old tin can of a piano that I had managed to get. Someone asked, 'Does anyone dance?' and one said 'Yes, I can' and got on a table and danced to 'You are my lucky star'. The patients missed their families. Some had relatives who were prisoners of war, some had children. Sometimes they dare not ask about the post.

No one had leave on Christmas Day or Boxing Day. There was nowhere to go, anyway. By 8 o'clock the patients were all tired and ready for bed. Lights were out by 10 pm and then we went home to recover. My day had started before 7 am but it was worth all the work. The day belonged to the patients. I had bribed Mrs Fraser to keep me two ducks and we all sat down about 10 pm to Christmas dinner at the farm, including people from the dispensary and people with nowhere to go.

Reporting Christmas
by Monica Dickens

After a spell as junior reporter at the Hertfordshire Express, *Monica Dickens wrote the novel* My Turn to Make the Tea *based on her experiences at the newspaper's offices at Hitchin. At Christmas, her duties included visiting local hospital wards and reporting the concert at a local mental asylum. This extract from* My Turn to Make the Tea *by Monica Dickens (copyright the estate of Monica Dickens, 1951) is reproduced by permission of PFD (www.pfd.co.uk) on behalf of the estate of Monica Dickens.*

I stayed to see the staff concert. I had read and imagined a lot about the horrors of asylums, but Sister Taylor singing 'Bless this House' in a different key to the piano, wildly thumping to try and bring her into line, was the only horror I encountered at the Northgate.

Afterwards, there was old-fashioned dancing. I stood with the assistant matron and watched the patients dancing the barn dance and the Valeta and the Boston two-step. They seemed to enjoy these more than the ballroom dancing, and executed the various movements with concentration and grave skill. One woman, however, with basin-cut grey hair and a parakeet-coloured dress too short for her square figure, was very hysterical about the barn dance. She kept trying to order the other dancers about, and then going the wrong way herself and getting lost in the middle of the set, throwing it into chaos, and prancing about with her knees very high and her elbows stuck out. At the end of the dance, she panted: 'Lovely, lovely!' clapped her hands, grabbed a man who was walking away for a rest, and swung him abandonedly into the Valeta.

I knew there were many insane women in this hall, but she was the only one who really looked it.

'Er – that lady in a bright dress,' I asked the assistant matron. 'She seems – poor thing – I mean, I suppose she's one of the worst cases – ?'

'She,' said the assistant matron, 'has been sent from the occupational therapy centre to teach the patients old-fashioned dancing.'

She turned away, so that I could not see whether she was smiling. In case she was not, I found a nurse and got myself let out of all the locked doors to where my bicycle waited in the cold beyond the potted plants.

Boxing Day found me still working. Someone had to go and write up the Boxing Day meet in the market square, and Victor had said: 'You're always talking about horses. You can jolly well go.'

I hoped it would freeze, but when I woke next morning the sleet had turned to rain, so hey for boot and saddle, a fine hunting morning, with the rain soaking down as if it would never leave off until it had settled us all in arks. Casubon was obliging again, so I hacked my mettlesome bicycle through the veiled streets to the market place, which was a dismal, steaming pit of horses with their tails tucked in against the rain, riders ditto, with white mackintoshes over habits, and spectators with their collars up.

Quite a crowd of townspeople had come to stare and try to stroke the hounds. They viewed the scene without envy, glad that they had not got to do it themselves, but glad that someone should uphold the old tradition, which they had been vaguely led to believe had made England what it was. Hunting, the rich man's sport, curiously

Ickleford Road, Hitchin, *c.* 1920.

inspired no anarchy. Out of the field, the hunting classes had had their day. They could not get servants, their homes were being sold for schools and institutions, no one called them Sir any more, and there were the oddest looking people nowadays in the Berkeley. But having achieved the bloodless revolution, the working man allowed them this small, picturesque pleasure, and rather liked to read in his paper in wartime that Major the Hon. Justin Ogilvy had gone into action blowing a hunting horn.

The other people on foot were the indefatigables, who had come in porkpie hats and indestructible clothes to dash about in cars to strategic points, and then wade over a ploughed field to stand in a gateway, waving to their mounted friends as they charged through and splashed them with mud, and telling the Master, who knew better, which way the fox had gone. They had brought friends who were staying with them over Christmas, because 'Everyone always goes to the Boxing Day meet.' No question of who wanted to and who did not, the friends had accepted the fate of their shoes and come partly to counteract last night's port, and partly because there was no fire lit in the drawing-room before lunch.

I wanted to speak to the Master, to get the Personal Touch, which was still my Mecca, whatever the others might say, or Mr Pellet's pencil might do. I found him struggling out of a small car, in a long camelhair coat, stamping about with his legs spread to get the feel of his boots.

I introduced myself, and he said 'Morning', and started to walk away to where a rat-faced groom was trying to keep more than two legs of his horse on the ground at the same time.

I followed the Master. 'Excuse me, sir, er –' What on earth could I ask him? He stopped, surprised to find me still there. 'Er – do you expect a good hunt to-day?'

'Can't tell. Scent's tricky.' He walked on.

'Have you had a good season so far?'

'So-so.'

'How many couples have you out to-day?'

'Well, count for yourself,' he grunted, but then took pity on me and paused. 'Nineteen and a half. Bitch pack.' He walked on. I followed him like an insect, tickling him with questions, and he kept brushing me off with impatient answers. He reached his horse, exchanged sour nods with the groom, and put a foot in the stirrup, while the animal went round in mad circles on the slippery cobbles. When he was up and his weight pressed the saddle on to its cold back, it became even madder, so I left him to his Goddams and went in search of further copy.

Christmas Chronicle

✠

Extracts from the Trewin's of Watford house magazine, The Chronicle, *for 1967 by kind permission of the John Lewis Partnership Archive Collection.*

This year we wrote to our Pensioners, inviting them to help us with the Christmas Chronicle by sharing some of their memories with us. We are delighted with the ready response which was forthcoming and hope that all our still-working Partners will enjoy sharing these reminiscences with us.

Mrs A. Carpenter, who used to work in the Restaurant Kitchens – and still comes in to help on Mondays – was known affectionately to almost everyone in the Branch simply as Alice. She recalls a Christmas when a flu epidemic decimated the kitchen staff until only she, Mrs Greenfield (now Section Manager of Separates) and one washer-up were left to help the Spanish Chef and Mr Adams to keep the Restaurant going. Mrs Carpenter also recalls decorating each year, a boar's head and chickens in aspic which were displayed in the Restaurant but her most amusing memory concerns an evening function, a dinner for a party of Express Dairy men.

This was in the days of the Queen's Pantry – where Alice began work as a fourteen year old. The kitchen where the food was prepared, was on the top floor and the old fashioned cooking ovens and stove were on the ground floor! On the evening of the Dairy men's dinner, while preparing the soup, Alice asked her staff if they could not smell burning – or was it perhaps paraffin? The staff said she was imagining things and the work continued. Suddenly there was a tremendous bang and, through the windows Alice saw the sky lit up with fire. The bakehouse windows soon cracked in the heat. Someone who was living above the Trewin's shop said that anyone in the back of the Queen's Pantry must get out at once so Alice ordered her staff out into Queens Road. The fire proved to be a very dangerous one, which burned all night and still needed firemen the next day, in a spirit factory which was on the present site of British Home Stores in Loates Lane. Part of this factory bordered the back way into Trewin's and the old Queen's Pantry. Alice and her evacuated staff were watching the fire from Queens Road when their Manager's father came along, demanding to know if they were aware that the Dairy men's reception was on – and why were they not inside, getting on with the cooking! 'I told him,' says Alice, 'that if a dinner was more important than a life – well he knew where the kitchen was!'

Soon the Express Dairy men began arriving and voiced the hope that whatever it was that was burning it was not their dinner! All ended well, however, and the kitchen party were eventually allowed back and worked to such good effect that the Dairy men got their dinner only a bare half an hour late.

It was this splendid spirit which Alice brought with her to the Partnership when the Queens Pantry was taken over by Trewin's.

Mr F. Masters [who was at one time in charge of the Dispatch Department at Trewin's] recalls playing Father Christmas for Trewin Brothers in 1919. Dressed in traditional robes Mr Masters 'arrived' at Watford High Street Station and was driven round the town in style, with his reindeer and bells, arriving at Trewin's in the early afternoon for the Grand Opening of the Bazaar and the Enchanted

Trewin's piece goods department, early 1930s. Courtesy of the John Lewis Parthership Archive Collection.

Grotto with its Caves. This occupied the whole of the basement floor and included a beautiful rockery, with flowers and ferns, clever lighting and the artificial caves. It could all be explored for sixpence with a handshake from Father Christmas included in the price. The Saturday afternoon crowds for this attraction were so terrific, says Mr Masters, that a policeman used to stand at the top of the stairs to maintain order!

Trewin Brothers at that time ran a Club into which their customers could pay whatever sums they could afford, to be spent, usually on toys, at Christmas. The Dispatch Department would work all day on the Sunday before Christmas to make sure that all deliveries were made in time. The deliveries were made by Trewin's one and only horse-drawn van for this was even earlier than that rather quaint looking three-wheeled motor vehicle which ushered out the horse and preceded the motorising of all our deliveries. Mr Masters remembers mornings when he literally could not get in to his Dispatch Department for doll's prams, trikes and toy pedal cars.

The Stain on the Ceiling

by John Hopkins

John Hopkins was inspired to write this imaginary ghost story (originally intended for reading aloud) when he and his wife Kathleen were renovating their house, No. 70 High Street, Standon, in the 1970s. There was one stain that was particularly difficult to remove. We take up the story as he hears a woman crying – but there is no one there.

It felt a bit spooky, standing there in a dark, empty room but after a moment or two of fright, I rationalised it. Any noise I'd heard had, in fact, come from the shop next door and unfamiliarity with the acoustics had made me think that it had been in our own house. I went downstairs, rather relieved, and it was then, just as I was locking the back door, that I noticed it for the first time – the reddish-brown stain on the plaster ceiling immediately below the bathroom. To be honest, at that time I didn't think much of it. I cursed the fact that I hadn't noticed it in time for it to be painted before the panelling was put on the walls and I resolved to paint it out on my next visit.

That was on the Sunday. I took some primer sealer and slapped a thick coat over the stain. Well, as you know, I'm a bit of a lazy beggar and I thought that if I eliminated just the stain, I could then paint the whole ceiling with Vymura later on and get away with just the one coat. Well now, since Kathleen's a bit of a stickler – more of a stickler than I am, anyway – for proper procedures in decorating – I didn't mention it. But it wasn't until the following Friday that I came out again, on my own, as Kathleen had gone Christmas shopping. I went straight through to the bar to check the ceiling. Well, there it was – the stain, still as plain as ever. I couldn't understand it. That primer sealer would normally cover anything. It was then that someone tapped on the back door. It was the old workman who'd been helping to repair the roof of the lean-to. I forget what he actually wanted – probably to use the toilet in the garden room, I expect. Anyway, something made me show him the stain. Perhaps I felt he would have some old craftsman's trick for covering it. But he just looked at it and shook his head. 'They didn't tell you, then, before you bought the place?'

'Tell me what?'

'About what happened. Oh, no, I can see they didn't.'

'What should they have told me?' To be honest, I vaguely thought he meant something to do with the plumbing, or the leaky pipes, or something.

'About Arabella Bramley.'

Who's Arabella Bramley?'

He didn't answer straight away, but pulled up the old beer crate I'd been standing on to paint the ceiling, and rolled himself a cigarette.

'Well, I've lived around here most of my life, but it was before my time. Before my father's time, but my granddad, he told me. The Bramleys, they had the big house down the lane, by the ford. Now, I'm talking about Queen Victoria's time, you understand. Oh, generations of them had lived there. Not nobility, you understand, but certainly local gentry. Now, Arabella was the only daughter. Oh, she was a beautiful girl. Rode well, when not many women rode at all. Belle of the ball, courted by all the local young squires. You know the kind. Apple of her parents' eyes, but wayward with it.

The ghostly grave of Arabella Bramley. Drawing by Ken Woodruff.

Anyway, to cut a long story short, she took a fancy to the son of a family that lived here, in this house, then. They were just farm labourers, they were. I'm not sure that they weren't even tenants of the Bramleys, but I don't know for certain. Anyway, it was young Arthur that Arabella wanted. Oh, I daresay they was in love and all that, but it drove her mother and father mad. They wouldn't hear of it. They tried bribing Arthur. They tried threatening him but he stood firm. Anyway, they got married and they came to live here, with Arthur's parents. That little room, you know, that's your bathroom now, that was where they slept. Hardly room to turn round in and not at all what young Arabella was used to. Arthur's parents didn't help much. They hated the idea of the marriage almost as much as Arabella's parents and they didn't exactly make her welcome. Still, she stuck it out and she never complained.

Well, as things went on, times got harder. Life on the land in them days was a chancy business and it wasn't really Arthur's fault that he lost his job. Give him his due, he tried at all the farms for miles around, tramping and trudging, but they wouldn't have him. His marrying Arabella made him pretty unpopular locally. Now at that time, we was fighting the Russians out in the Crimea and finally, in desperation Arthur went for a soldier. Well, at least he could send something home to Arabella and though his parents weren't kind, they wouldn't turn her out.

So that's how it was then, and the months passed. Then, one day, Arabella met up with one of her old beaux. Now, I don't want to blame the girl really. After all, her life was pretty miserable here. But you makes your bed and you lies on it, I say. Still, this young spark – my grandfather never said his name – he kept coming round and taking Arabella out in his carriage, and riding. He had a bachelor establishment over towards Albury End way and he took her there more than once. Well, you plays with fire and you're going to get burnt and, inevitably, young Arabella finished up in the family way – and that was the last she saw of her young fancy man. He was off out of it like a flash and poor Arabella had to live her life out.

Arthur's parents wouldn't have her downstairs. They wouldn't let her go out in case the neighbours saw her and they just left her food on the landing. Sometimes she'd walk in the little garden – well, it wasn't overlooked in those days. Well, she was miserable, but time passed and the baby was born, poor little perisher. Dead within the week. It was then that Arabella broke. All she did was cry and cry, sobbing her heart out in that there back room. Arthur's parents, they saw the Vicar – he was a decent fellow, he was, for them days – and they arranged for the baby to be buried in the churchyard in the corner, up on the hill there, at the back. Nobody spoke to Arabella. They just took the poor little mite's body away and she just cried

How long it would have gone on for, God knows, but it was only about two days after the baby's funeral – a week before Christmas, it was – that the letter came. From Arthur. He was on his way home. He'd made sergeant. Things should be better. That night, Arabella did it. She came downstairs to the kitchen, after her in-laws were asleep, took the long knife from the drawer back to her room and cut her wrists. Next morning, they found her. It was the blood on the ceiling beneath that made them go upstairs. She was dead, of course. There was nothing they could do. The Vicar came up trumps again. Suicides didn't always get a churchyard burial in them days. But if you go up the hill in the churchyard, you'll see the stones; Arabella's just with her name and dates and the little one by her side. All it says on that is 'An infant. Died 1856'.

That's more or less the end of the story. Arthur's parents scrubbed the floorboards clean. Clean and white they were, upstairs. But nothing they could do with whitewash or lime could ever get that there stain out.' He stubbed his cigarette out and stood up. 'Mind you, there's some that swears that every year, just before Christmas, you can hear Arabella sobbing and crying, but to my mind that's just imagination.'

Dark Streets Shining

by Margaret Ashby

O, little town of Bethlehem, how still we see thee lie!
Above thy deep and dreamless sleep, the silent stars go by.
Yet in thy dark streets shineth the everlasting light;
The hopes and fears of all the years are met in thee tonight.

I was seven the Christmas we learnt 'O, Little town of Bethlehem'. It was the winter of 1947, bleak, cold and cheerless. St Nicholas' School, built in 1832, still retained its latched doors, coke fires and draughts.

In Stevenage, in 1947, there was little in the way of Christmas sparkle. Nothing could dim the relief that the War was over but, as well as the fervent hopes for a lasting peace, the fears and sorrows which the War had engendered were still about us, emphasized by the shortages, the drabness and general weariness as well as the depressing news, little understood by children, from far away countries. Clothes and sweets were still rationed and few goods were obtainable in the shops. If we were lucky enough to receive a parcel through the post, we carefully undid the string and unwrapped the brown paper for future use. Often it had been in service several times before, as witnessed by a number of carefully crossed out addresses.

Years later, when shops were better stocked, I was amazed to discover that one could actually buy new brown paper and string. I still cannot cut string and continue to save it in untidy little skeins for

future use. Christmas wrapping paper was even more precious and was re-used until it fell apart. In our house, any salvaged wrapping paper was smoothed out, carefully folded and put away in the cupboard under the stairs for next year. Buying new paper nowadays always reminds me of the thrill of the crumpled, second-hand holly patterned paper of childhood.

Parcels and letters were posted at one of a row of seventeenth-century buildings at the south end of the High Street. Officially the South End Post Office, it was known to everyone as 'Miss Norman's'. Entry was up two high steps, through the door which always first stuck then burst open, causing a tinny bell to ring. Inside, it was brown and tiny, with room for about six people standing. The smell was unforgettable, compounded of ink, gum and mysterious Post Office stationery, clean and unsentimental. On the left was a high, brown varnished counter behind which Miss Norman presided and beyond, a glimpse of her little sitting room with its photograph, on the round table in the window, of a handsome man in uniform. Brother? Lover killed in the War?

Facing the shop door was a wooden shelf containing blotting paper, inkwells and two dipper pens for those who needed to sign documents. Another shelf, above it, held a few items of stationery for sale. The wall to the right was papered with instructive notices, urging the young to buy National Savings stamps. A magnificent poster on the back of the door warned of imminent invasion by the Colorado Beetle. As a child, waiting patiently for grown-up business to be transacted or, less patiently, for grown-up gossip to end – in those days shopping was less to do with buying things than with social intercourse – I had ample opportunity to study the pictures of the Colorado Beetle. Despite the detailed instructions about how to identify the creature, how to trap it in a match box and where to take it when thus safely caged, the poster failed to disclose the nature of the crime it had committed.

In the weeks before Christmas there would be many a visit, in the twilight of a December afternoon, to Miss Norman's. There were letters to send to cousins serving in the forces overseas; stamps to be bought; parcels to be sent, with much agonising as to whether registered or not, to aunts and uncles; and possibly, some last minute cards to be purchased. Buying cards from Miss Norman was not easy for a child. Firstly, there was the problem of seeing over the tall counter. The second and more difficult hurdle, was her kindly interrogation, 'Who is it for? Your Auntie!' A pause, while she opened a drawer behind the counter and flicked through her stock, finally selecting one, 'Here you are, Auntie will like this one.' Sometimes I was brave enough to reject her choice and ask to see another and once I even tried to persuade her to let me look through the whole drawerful, but this was not allowed. Only grown-ups were given unrestricted access to the hoard.

Outside, in the gloom, the High Street was dark: a few street lights had reappeared now that the need for black-out was over, but their glow was feeble. Most shops, despite their proprietors' best efforts, contributed little by way of festive decor. To me, the most dismal section of all was Middle Row. Its cobbles and old buildings were dilapidated and grimy. There were some shops, including Halling's neatly-painted butcher's, but mostly Middle Row was divided into cottages, whose front doors opened immediately on to the street. I had fearful visions of what they must be like inside, dark, pokey, low-ceilinged and primitive, I imagined. In the winter, when it was dusk as we came home from school I was often scared to walk through

Middle Row. Drawing by Ken Woodruff.

Middle Row because it was so dark and mysterious.

At school we were learning carols. Each class learned a new one every year, starting with 'Away in a Manger' for the five year olds and progressing to all kinds of mysteries by the age of eleven. The previous year I had missed out completely, having spent weeks at home with a succession of feverish illnesses which had culminated just before Christmas in a gruesome three days in hospital to have my tonsils removed. In 1947, however, I was in better health and I was in Mrs Ives' class. She was a good teacher, being firm enough to keep order but not so strict as to frighten us into dumbness.

Patiently, Mrs Ives taught us all four verses of 'O, Little Town of Bethlehem', writing each line on the blackboard, explaining the difficult words and drawing out the meaning of obscure phrases. She tried to help us imagine the dark and huddled streets of an eastern town, where there were no lights but the stars. All that came into my mind's eye were the dark and huddled buildings of Middle Row. Mrs Ives told us of a wicked world in which the Jewish people were oppressed and evil and cruelty were all about. We were too young to understand fully, but we knew from the shadows in grown-up eyes as they listened to the news on the wireless, that evil still abounded.

I did not quite understand 'the hopes and fears of all the years' but somehow those words seemed right for the times we lived in and, running home from school through the winter dusk, with the carol singing in my head, I knew that here, at Christmas, the everlasting light would shine in Middle Row's dark street.

Bygrave Christmas
by Margaret Ashby

As the grey murk which had passed for daylight finally faded into darkness, the mobile library van trundled towards its last stop of the day.

Our Irish driver was prepared for the worst, 'If the fog gets really thick, ye'll have to get out and walk ahead with a torch to show me the road, Peg,' he said. 'Tie a piece of string to the bumper and hold the other end so that ye don't lose me.' Praying that the mist would not get any worse, I listened gloomily to reminiscences of fogs encountered, of near disasters and miraculous escapes. Through the windscreen we could see little of the north Hertfordshire countryside; the arc of our headlights showed an empty road, a hedge or a fence and occasionally a cottage. Beyond, all was blackness, no lights shone, no stars; even cottage windows were dull and shrouded against the December night.

We were like aliens exploring a strange planet (though this was 1959 and men had not yet reached the moon), safe as long as we stayed in our vehicle, but surrounded by a vast nothingness. Or so it appeared. In reality we were less than a dozen miles from Baldock, Letchworth and Hitchin, where there were street lights and traffic and people rushing about in a frenzy of last minute Christmas shopping, but so remote were we in our fearful isolation that I could not make the connection.

The whole day had been grey, the mist separating us from

normality. The seasonal bustle which was taking place in the towns had seduced most of our readers and this usually pleasant route had seemed dreary and pointless. At Radwell, the tiny Domesday village beside the Great North Road, no one wanted library books this week. Perhaps they had even forgotten that we were coming. I gazed at the moorhens on the lake, but for once did not feel my customary thrill of pleasure at being in this remote and ancient corner of the county.

We had driven back to the main road and through the lanes towards Newnham and Hinxworth. Usually I enjoyed driving through these northern extremities of Hertfordshire, through a landscape left untouched for centuries with sweeping open fields and scattered woods. Today, all was dismal, earth and sky merging into gloom. There seemed to be no life anywhere, no twittering flocks of sparrows and finches and no sign of the pursuing sparrowhawk that we occasionally saw here, flying low and parallel with the van.

At Newnham there had been a little more activity. One or two people were about in the village and we had a basket of books returned by an emissary from the Rectory who wished us a happy Christmas and commiserated about the weather, though in the rather preoccupied manner of one who has a cake to ice.

Hinxworth is so near the county boundary that people often walked from the neighbouring Bedfordshire village of Edworth to borrow books from our van. This was not officially approved, but we pretended not to notice their address. Hinxworth people were very hospitable, one lady even insisting on inviting us in for tea and scrambled egg on toast on each of our fortnightly calls. Today had been no exception and, cheered by her hospitality, we had gone out again into the dark, empty village street and turned the van towards Ashwell.

Bygrave church. Photograph by M. Ashby.

Now something of a tourist village, noted for its old pargeted houses in the High Street, its village museum and its magnificent church with the famous graffito of old St Paul's cathedral, Ashwell in the middle ages was a market town, the centre of an important corn-growing area. I always enjoyed driving along the High Street, then into Bear Lane and Silver Street, pondering on the origins of the names. 'Silver' clearly came from the Latin for 'a wood' but 'Bear' offered interesting speculations. Today, even Ashwell had seemed dull and gave no sign that Christmas was so near.

It was late afternoon now and we drove on, into the increasing gloom, heading towards Bygrave, another of those tiny villages of north Hertfordshire. A relic of a more prosperous past, Bygrave with its ancient church of St Margaret of Antioch, now stands almost alone in the wide, unenclosed fields.

The next stop would be our last for the day. We turned off the Baldock road into Wedon Way, an unmade-up road warningly labelled 'Unadopted', and bumped and rattled over its rough surface. Although the houses here were modern, there were no street lights and when we switched off our engine we were in a silent, black world. I thought, 'This is a complete waste of time. No one wants us. What a miserable, bleak day it has been – not a bit like Christmas.'

Suddenly, a front door burst open and a little girl, about ten years of age, skipped and danced towards us. 'Mummy, mummy, it's the library. The library van is here.' Behind her, in the bright hallway of the house, was a Christmas tree with tinsel and coloured lights sparkling, transforming the night. So, centuries ago, must the ancient church of St Margaret of Antioch sparkled with light and colour, its wall paintings and holy images lit by candles and burning oil lights. So must the cold, dark nights of medieval Bygrave have been illuminated by the warmth and brilliance of the church.

A young woman with a serene, smiling face followed the child out, laughing lovingly at her daughter's excitement, putting a gentle hand on her shoulder. We stood talking quietly in the darkness, our eyes drawn to the light flooding from the open doorway, our hearts warmed by the glow of Christmas in Wedon Way, Bygrave.

A Cottage Christmas
by Edwin Grey

Cottage Life in a Hertfordshire Village, *from which this extract is taken, is widely admired as a classic account of rural life. Edwin Grey was born in Harpenden in 1859, began work at the nearby Rothamsted Experimental Station when he was thirteen and, in the words of Sir E. John Russell, 'by sheer merit, worked his way up to the post of Field Superintendent'. Cottage Life in a Hertfordshire Village was published by Fisher, Knight & Co. Ltd of St Albans in 1934. Permission to reprint this extract was given by Edwin Grey's nephew, Reginald Bath.*

When about eight or nine years old, I remember being invited to spend Christmas with my uncle, aunt and cousins, at a cottage on the outskirts of the parish; there were four children in the family, one boy and three girls, my uncle being a gardener; here we had a small but real fir Christmas tree provided. I do not recollect seeing any fancy boxes of chocolates, nor bonbons, on the tree, but I remember that besides its adornment of Christmas candles, fruit, figures and flags, there were a number of little satchets or dorothy bags, which the girls had made out of odd pieces of coloured silk or other dress material. These dainty little bags were filled, some with nuts and almonds, others with various sorts of sweets, etc, which were eventually cut from the tree and distributed among us. The whole tree was further adorned by ropes of scarlet holly berries, threaded singly on long lengths of thread. These ropes of scarlet berries were tied, looped and festooned about the tree, giving a very pretty effect when the candles were lighted up. Bigger and older boys and girls told of the Christmas tree treats that used to be given to the scholars attending the Church Sunday School, these being held in the National Schoolroom. I understood that the trees and presents were mainly the gift of the Misses Wilson, who at that time lived at Welcombe (now St Dominic's Convent). I do not remember these good ladies, for by the time I can clearly remember they had left the village, 'scared away', so the cottagers said, by the advent of the new railroad, which skirted their private grounds at the back of the house, thus I suppose sadly disturbing the hitherto quiet peacefulness of their home and surroundings. These ladies must have been much beloved by the cottagers of this district, for even now they are spoken of with affection by old cottagers who knew them; there were other ladies too, whose memory is still treasured with deep affection and respect, more so perhaps by the older cottagers of this southern part of the parish; among them the late Mrs Warde of 'Bennetts', Miss Miller of 'The Dene', Mrs Tylston Hodgson of 'Welcombe', Lady Gilbert (then Mrs Gilbert) of the 'Laboratory House', Miss Taylor of 'River's Lodge', and others. But of all these good ladies, the memory of the late Mrs Warde (sister of the late Sir John Lawes), is still held in the deepest affection; most of the cottagers of those days when speaking to or of her would address her as Lady Warde or My Lady, and although Mrs Warde herself would often correct them, saying that 'Lady' was not her title, yet they would persist in so doing, and those old surviving cottagers who knew her, still speak of her as 'Lady Warde'. It was owing to his lady's influence and help, that many a cottage boy and girl from this part of the parish was given a good start on the road to a successful career.

Cottage life, 1881.

I cannot remember any members of this agricultural community visiting very far afield but as always has been the custom at Christmastide, children endeavoured to pay a visit to parents, or vice versa, and friend call upon friend at this festive season. These visits entailed no great preparations, for the majority of relatives and friends lived in the near vicinity, or within the boundary of the parish, others would be mostly living in the surrounding villages and hamlets, generally within what was deemed to be easy walking distances, for in those days a walk of six or seven miles each way on a Sunday or Christmas Day visit was thought nothing of. A cottager would sometimes during the summer months take one or two of his children with him for a treat, when making a parental visit to one or other of these aforesaid villages; I knew older children who have told how they had been taken by their father on a Sunday visit to their grandparents, and that they had walked the six miles or more each way. The little party would start after breakfast taking the nearest cuts by footpaths and by-lanes, well known to the man, reaching their destination before dinner, starting on the homeward journey soon after tea.

I remember one of the labourers who was working on the Experimental Plots, telling me one day of a friend of his who used sometimes on a Sunday to walk over to Bedmond to visit some friends there (this village lies about seven or eight miles to the S.W. of Harpenden), and that his friend used to take a near cut through Childwick Park; sometimes if the weather was fine and the grass dry he would leave the footpath and make a still nearer cut across the Park. One Sunday morning when he was so doing he was met by Squire Lomax, the then owner of Childwick Bury, when the following conversation took place.

Home for Christmas, 1880s.

The Squire: 'Where are you going?'

The man: 'I'm goin' ter me friends, sur.'

The Squire: 'What do you do, and how do you manage at your friends?'

The man: 'Well, sur, they finds th' grub, an' I finds th' beer.'

The Squire: 'Ah well, there's no doubt but that the beer costs far the most, so I shall not come with you, but anyhow in the future when you go to see your friends, you must keep to the footpath.'

There's no doubt but that the new railway offered attractive holiday programmes at all festive seasons, but being then only a small boy, I was not old enough to know anything about it, but however, neither week-end, bank, or any other holiday (save that of Christmas Day, and maybe the annual club feast dinners) was for the agricultural worker as yet, and as neither the Midland nor the Great Northern Railway served directly any of the surrounding villages save that of Wheathampstead, the farm labourer, when visiting relatives or friends residing in one or the other of the somewhat isolated villages or hamlets around, nearly always did the journey on foot (often termed as Shank's pony), for other means of getting there were, as a rule, beyond his purse. However, I never knew any of the farm men at all envious of a more fortunate neighbour who might perchance be able to take a week-end or perhaps a longer holiday. 'I don't want ter goo gaddin' about, a tiring yerself putty well ter death. I'd rather be 'arf ev a 'our or tew on me garden, an' a pint or tew o' beer,' I've heard men say at times, when the talk was turned on holiday making. Neither do I as a boy clearly remember the carols at Christmastide (for, of course, there was carol singing then as always), but I recollect a bit later the excellent carol party, the members of which were both sexes, who, under the leadership of the late Tom

Lovett (the village crier) went round to the more important houses in the near neighbourhood at this season 'carol singing'; the members of this party were mainly from the cottage homes comprising the groups and cottage colonies of this southern part of the parish; all these selected members possessed very fine voices, and they took their parts and sang their carols unaccompanied. I remember also the clever company of handbell ringers (called the Harpenden Handbell Ringers) the members of which were mainly from the village proper; this party of handbell ringers under the directorship of the late Mr H. Child, Snr (the owner of the bells) also at the Christmas season, performed at the chief residences in the neighbourhood. An old custom observed in my boyhood days was that of 'Going a Thomasing'. I knew several elderly widows, who each year on the feast of 'St Thomas' (December 21) would go round to some of the principal houses in the neighbourhood 'a Thomasing'. The women that I knew, always called at the same houses and were evidently expected, for they told me they always got a 'somethin' at each place of call, one gentleman gave a new sixpence each year to every 'Thomaser' calling at his home. I asked what they said or did when calling at the houses. Said they: 'All we ses is "please we've cum a Thomasing, remember St Thomas's day"'.

On Christmas Eve
by James Smith

The writings of James Smith, edited by David Perman, were published under the title A Quaint Old Fashioned Place *by Hertfordshire Publications in 1990. Smith wrote the rather gloomy short story from which this extract is taken after he had emigrated to Australia, but it is redolent of his youth in east Hertfordshire. It was first published in 1880.*

The month of December, 18--, was gloomier, if possible than that season usually is in England. For days together a dense and chilly fog hung over the valley of the Lea, blotting out the landscape and intercepting the weak watery sunshine from the miry roads and sodden paths. The dull, heavy, depressing atmosphere was well calculated to fill my mind with sombre thoughts and desponding feelings. The long dark nights were succeeded by short and cheerless days, during which you seemed to be living in a misty twilight that was terribly monotonous in its dreary sadness. And all the while I resembled those of whom it was written – 'Thy life shall hang in doubt before thee... In the morning thou shalt say, Would God it were even! and at even thou shalt say, Would God it were morning! for the fear of thy heart wherewith thou shalt fear'.

Evening after evening, as we sat by the fireside, my aunt Janet would enlarge upon the affectionate forethought of my deceased father, the one object of whose life she asserted to have been the accumulation of a fortune for my inheritance, and upon the attractive person and excellent qualities of my cousin, whom I had not seen since she was a child. And then the strong-willed woman would take my hand in one of hers, lay the other on my head, and look me continuously in the eyes until I became conscious that I was thinking her thoughts, being swayed by her feelings, and yielding myself an unwilling servitor to her imperious will. At that time, as I have said, I was entirely ignorant of the phenomena of electro-biology and animal magnetism: but my aunt, as I afterwards learnt, had spent a good many years of her life in Germany, where she had become familiar with those phenomena, and had acquired the knowledge of her own 'will-power'.

At length the leaden feet of Time crept on to Christmas Eve, and on the day following I was to make my irrevocable decision. How well I remember that eventful night! The wind had gone round to the North soon after daybreak, and a soft but steady fall of snow had come down with a gentle hush upon the bare brown earth, transforming every object it enveloped in its pure white shroud. It lay like a robe of stainless fleece on tree and shrub, and it spread a pavement of radiant smoothness, that glittered in the sunshine as though it were composed of the marble Pentelicus, over the flat and marshy pastures in the valley of the Lea. I endeavoured to beguile the weary hours by assisting my aunt in decorating the church with holly, bay-leaves, and ivy for the Christmas festival, our own shrubberies providing us with plenty of material for the purpose; but my trouble accompanied me wherever I went and in whatever I did.

Night came, and with it the children of the village school, huddling beneath the shelter of the porch, and singing the old old carols, orally handed down from generation to generation and bearing traces in their composition of their Roman Catholic origin. Besides receiving a gift of money, the little choristers were regaled with mulled elder wine, and toast, and cake and sent upon their way rejoicing. Even the grim features of my aunt relaxed into a smile as she saw the ruddy countenances of the red-cloaked itinerants glow with the warmth influxed into their systems by the hot wine, and heard the outspoken expressions of their enjoyment. When I bade her good-night she gave me her cheek to kiss – I had never known her to do so since I was a child – and briefly said, 'Tomorrow, Herbert'. I merely nodded in reply, and turned away with a heavy heart, and a heavier step. I lay awake until midnight, tossing and tumbling in a fever of unrest. Then I heard the fine peal of bells in the Church of St Mary, in the neighbouring town of Ware, shake forth a softened stream of music on the still and silent air, and, mechanically repeating these lines from 'In Memoriam', I fell into a deep sleep:

> This year I slept and woke with pain,
> I almost wished no more to wake,
> And that my hold on life would break
> Before I heard those bells again.
>
> But they my troubled spirit rule,
> For they controlled me when a boy;
> They bring me sorrow touched with joy,
> The merry merry bells of Yule.

'The Silent Snows', a Victorian engraving.

Victorian Christmas Fare
by Gerald Curtis

The brewer John Izzard Pryor retired to Clay Hall, Walkern in 1828 and for the next thirty years kept careful records of his activities. Reproduced from Gerald Curtis: A Chronicle of Small Beer: The Early Victorian Diaries of a Hertfordshire Brewer *(1970) by permission of the publisher, Phillimore, of Shopwyke Manor Barn, Chichester, West Sussex, England.*

Christmas Day, 1842

Our Christmas Party consisted of sons John, Morris, Alfred and Fred... A very fine cod, boiled turkey and four very fine ribs of beef, fatted by my brother Vickris, being the choicest of the lot sent up from Herefordshire to tie up, about two months since.

Christmas Day, 1843

The party at dinner 11. Cod fish and oysters from Buisses. Spent a pleasant evening. Mr and Mrs Harding left at about 11 o'clock and soon after 12 we five men, after the ladies had retired, sat down to a game of vingt et une [*sic*] at which I was a considerable winner – a very unusual thing for me. Finished with oysters and Hatfield ale and broke up about two in he morning.

The supremacy of the cod was challenged when the development of railways made available a greater variety of sea fish:

December 24, 1852

Received by rail this day a turbot and lobsters, a crimped cod, and two barrels of oysters from Pitmans.

Christmas Day, 1852

Our rector and his wife joined our party as usual for our Christmas dinner. Had a fine turbot with lobster sauce, soup, boiled turkey and roast ribs of beef.

December 26, 1852

All met again at dinner, partook of a crimped cod, oyster sauce, giblet soup and a new haunch of small mutton with sundries.

Plum pudding probably formed a part of the Christmas dinner, but was not considered important enough by John Izzard to mention. It will be noticed that he says nothing about the sweet course.

Every Christmas he gave the farm men a dinner of boiled beef and plum pudding. It is doubtful, however, whether plum pudding had as yet acquired its present status of a dish which is eaten only at Christmastide. It will be remembered that it formed part of the dinner which he gave to Dear Fred and his little friends when they played cricket at Clay Hall on 10 July 1830.

The giving of presents formed no part of the Early Victorian Christmas except that those in a position to do so, might send items of Christmas fare such as a cod fish, a barrel of oysters, game or poultry or a kild of ale to less favoured members of the community. John Izzard always sent a barrel of oysters to Farmers Rowlatt and Stacey of Walkern.

The following is the first reference to a Christmas present:

Victorian Christmas fare. Drawing by Ken Woodruff.

December 26, 1844

Presented six pocket books to my wife, children, and grand-children, writing their names in each. Son Alfred and his wife joined our party this afternoon. All our beds are now fully occupied and every stall in our stables.

It will be noticed that the pocket books were given, not on Christmas Day, but on Boxing Day, and appear to have been given to his wife, his daughters Emma and Eliza Lafont and her three children.

Next year he gave presents on New Year's Day:

January 1, 1845

Made presents to my grand children accompanied by a verse of poetry to Marian and Winifred.

Christmas Day, 1848

Dr and Mrs Bliss, my wife and daughter went in the omnibus to church. I walked but found it rather dirty. I found by my place in our pew a very handsome, or rather elegant Prayer Book, a Christmas present from Dr Bliss which I shall value much.

There was no Christmas tree at Clay Hall in John Izzard's time, but regularly every year he used to supply one to Mrs Malet, the wife of the Puseyite vicar of Ardeley:

Christmas Eve, 1852

Selected a spruce tree for Mrs Malet's Christmas family party which she decorates with fancy lamps for the occasion. Their servant came over with a little cart to fetch it.

A Memory of
Christmas at Hatfield
by Lady Hardinge of Penshurst

Lady Hardinge was born Helen Cecil. This article, from a talk broadcast on the BBC Home Service, was first published in The Listener *of 25 December 1958. Permission to reprint extracts here has been given by the author's grandson, Lord Hardinge of Penshurst.*

I remember, as a child, sitting on the stairs of my home quietly weeping, and my father asking 'What's the matter?' I said: 'I think I want to go to Hatfield.'

Hatfield House spelt happiness for me especially at Christmas. My memory of arriving there is clear but odd. I have no recollection of the journey until our horse's hooves crunched on the gravel of the north front. I was met off the train by a one-horse brougham. From the railway side the large Tudor house showed as a dark mass against the evening sky. Then round the west wing, with me in a state of mounting excitement, to the quadrangle of the south front, where the building blazed with light. I would look up to the first floor windows of the long gallery running the length of the house, to see the gold ceiling reflected in light. I felt as if powerful angelic wings might be bearing me aloft instead of my quietly descending from the brougham to the gentle attentiveness of old servants; and then climbing the stairs, where the true fragrance of the house reached me: the beautiful old woods and the panelling combined with the warmth of the house to give out lovely subtle and varied scents.

The Cecil cousins were long and lanky; animated in discussion or withdrawn when checked by a point that needed rethinking. But in spite of the noise and heat of argument I never heard a voice raised in anger in that house. We had complete freedom except that we were not free to be rude. No ill-considered statement passed unchallenged. One thing that made Hatfield so distracting and delicious was that conversation was not ruled by age: you were allowed to speak and taken seriously, however young you were. The youngest member of the family, for instance, might be heard saying: 'I would much rather Disraeli had not been Prime Minister. He was a great author and his being Prime Minister was a waste of time – someone else could have done that! No one else could write his books'.

After breakfast on Christmas Eve we all collected round the tree and began decorating. Too-great individualists, unless they had decorative genius, did their work at the back of the tree because the front must be an achievement; and all must go to its glory. The decorating took all the morning. After lunch there was talk round the long gallery fires, then an excursion to help my uncle build a bonfire and light it far off in the garden – a splendid occupation. We got gloriously dirty and, returning, changed into tidy clothes. In a ceremonial evening hour, in darkness, the tree – on a marble dais – was lit and shed its magic beauty along the chequered floor. It was transformed from its overdressed daylight appearance – transformed and radiant.

The hall was full of people come together for the rejoicings. There were trestle tables down its length with presents on. The distribution of these was supervised by my best-beloved aunt, assisted by us. This necessitated finding individuals in the dark hall. The dummy men-at-arms held dim red lanterns only, and by this faint illumination, slightly reflected in the marble floor, one was expected to find 'Old Mrs. Smith – *you* know – the one who lives in "New Town"!' At the foot of the tree there was light and bustle and parcels being given and received. But the best of all was when the choir in the hall sang 'Noel'. There was stillness for this as the sweet, pure voices rose in songs of adoration, and for me this moment held beauty and eternity. I would stand by my aunt. She had the richest personality and sense of humour I ever met.

There was a quietness now until dinner: dinner in the big dining-room, from the gallery of which hung Napoleon's Waterloo eagles, and from whose panelled walls Queen Elizabeth, her gown covered in eyes and ears, watched us eating an enormous meal, of which she herself would have thought nothing. Late to bed, happily talking and dawdling was a delight. Thoughts and joys expanded in the unrestricted atmosphere. Nobody said 'Do hurry!' 'Why are you making such a noise?', 'Why don't you say something?', or 'Why don't you shut up?'

On Christmas morning, darkness outside, in the chapel candlelight and kneeling figures, and once more before God. All the faculties of those present were absorbed in dedication. So many different strong personalities in humble adoration of the Saviour. It was not just habit and beautiful words, it was for us our hold on unending life and our strength on earth. After the service we would go to the library. There was an upper gallery, where one could sit and listen to the talk of one's elders in the room below, or read one's book instead.

On going up to one's room, one was apt to get stuck in the

Detail from a watercolour of Queen Victoria and guests in the long gallery at Hatfield House, 1846. Courtesy of the Marquess of Salisbury.

lift. The lift had been one of the earliest electric ones. It bore a resemblance to – but was less reliable than – the chariot which took Elijah aloft, and being unable to rise straight to heaven through the lead roof, it remained stuck there. Or, you pressed a button and sailed upwards to midway between the two top floors. There you stopped. This experience would upset visitors. It did not upset my aunt. There was a seat in the lift and she always had her correspondence with her and would settle down to deal with it until rescued.

There is little more that I could say of my childhood's visits to this house of abiding happiness: the whirling dances in the long gallery; the sight of two cousins, a brother and sister, waltzing in harmony – tall, graceful, spinning, endlessly remote in companionable silence. Music, light, swirling movement, life and laughter – the high gold ceiling above all: the great windows uncurtained, framing the stars beyond; the glorious warmth of the rooms.

There, I learned about politics, science, the stars, the universe, and the glory of God, from listening to the witty conversation of all my relations. It was there that I learned of the strong spiritual forces which rule men's hearts; there that I learned to love and enjoy life.

Frost on ivy leaves. Photograph by M. Ashby

Christmas Past in Buntingford
by Philip Plumb

First published in the Buntingford Journal, *Vol. 12 No. 10, and reprinted here by kind permission of the author.*

One of the features of Christmas past in Buntingford was the Christmas Fat Stock Show as remembered by the late Bert Thody in the parish magazine in December 1960. This was in the days when there was a weekly Monday market on Market Hill and the Show attracted buyers and spectators from a wide area. In 1928, when the Show was in its prime, 74 head of cattle were tied to rails on the wide part of the hill opposite Barclays Bank and 168 sheep and 250 pigs were penned on the cement under the trees. Turkeys and hens were on show in the tanyard (by then disused) and there was a display of roots in the Foresters Hall, next to the Post Office.

The prize beast was a black Aberdeen Angus from Mr Jack Russell of Alswick Hall, which was bought by High Street butcher, Mr H.W. Piggott, for £59. The pubs were open from early morning, as they were every Monday, for the refreshment of sellers and buyers alike. During the evening over 70 farmers and buyers sat down to an Old English Dinner at the George Hotel under the chairmanship of Major M.E. Barclay, MFH. When Bert Thody asked Sid Howlett, another Buntingford butcher who had also acted as a cattle grader for the Ministry since 1939 at many local markets, what the Prize Beast would have fetched in 1960, the answer was about £180.

Christmas for those who were children in the town just before the Second World War started in 1939 was marked colourfully by the festive displays in the shops. Moss's (in the building now the Library) which was owned by the International Stores Group but retained its original name, was crammed from floor to ceiling with seasonable goods: Christmas cakes, puddings, biscuits in fancy boxes (the tins of broken biscuits sold very cheaply were put out of sight for the season), Christmas decorations and everything for the occasion.

The newspaper shop, A.G. Day, also sold toys all the year round but at Christmas opened up a rear stock room (the actual shop was much shallower than now) as an Aladdin's cave of a toy showroom. Children were allowed in, under supervision, to gaze excitedly at the glittering display and to mentally reserve those they hoped to find in the Christmas stocking, or perhaps pillowcase.

Brown's Xmas Bazaar was a counter attraction at the other end of the High Street. This was a draper's shop in what is now the bookshop and hairdresser's opposite Market Hill and at Christmas time a variety of toys was displayed in its ample windows; boxed games, sets of Britain's lead soldiers, a castle or two for them to fight over, dolls and stuffed toys and other desirable things.

Going back in time to Christmas 1930, the *Buntingford and North East Herts Gazette*, a weekly forerunner of the *Journal*, recorded in its issues of December 26th and January 2nd a very busy festive season. There had been a carol concert at Tyneholme private school; a carol service at St Peter's Church in which the Layston Sunday School children had been strengthened with adult voices; a Christmas panto in the Benson Hall – *Dick Whittington* in the week following Christmas; and even a Christmas ghost had been seen by some lads

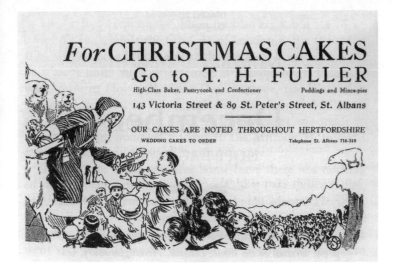

Advertisement for Fuller's cakes, 1930s.

in Chapel End which attracted the London press to send down their reporters but without a reappearance.

The villagers of Aspenden were treated to their traditional Christmas dinner by Sir Arthur and Lady Lushington with entertainment by the Buntingford Silver Band and a conjuror. The less fortunate inmates of the Bridgefoot House Institution were, as at every Christmas, given a hearty breakfast, a sumptuous Christmas dinner with all the trimmings, and a huge tea, all provided by the Guardians. Despite all this food they then entertained themselves, almost everyone doing a turn including one lady of 91 who sang several old time songs.

A Military Christmas
by Chris Reynolds

First published in the Hertfordshire Countryside *magazine for December 1995 and reprinted here by permission of the author, the following article is based on Chapter 18 of the book* The London Gunners Come to Town; life and death in Hemel Hempstead in the Great War *by Bertha and Chris Reynolds, published in 1995 by Codil Language Systems Ltd, Tring.*

The Terriers were not pleased. It was Christmas and all home leave had been cancelled.

Four months earlier, in August 1914, the men of the Second London Division, Territorial Force, had marched north to their War Stations in Hertfordshire. The Divisional headquarters were set up in the Peahen Hotel in St Albans and over 15,000 troops were billeted in the town or the surrounding countryside in an area stretching from Watford to Harpenden. While the majority of the troops were infantry men, the cavalry, in the form of King Edward's Horse, were based at Hunton Bridge, while the mounted Cyclists' Battalion could be found at Redbourn. Two brigades of gunners were stationed in or around Hemel Hempstead old town, another was at Boxmoor, while the howitzers and heavy guns ended up in the Apsley and Kings Langley area.

When they first arrived the talk had been that the war would be over by Christmas – but news from France soon showed that this was not to be. In fact three battalions of infantry, the London Scottish from North Watford, the Kensingtons from the Abbots Langley area, and the Queen's Westminster Rifles from Leverstock Green, were already fighting in the trenches and had been replaced by other territorials from the London Regiment.

During the autumn they had trained hard, with drills and route marches. There were skirmishes on Berkhamsted Common, and on the banks of the river Chess somewhere between Sarratt and Chorleywood. A large scale exercise in December involved supposed enemy troops to the East of Sandridge, while the following week a combined force had to take a crossing over the river at Kings Langley. While the men were all waiting for the opportunity to do their bit in the war, they were hoping for a final Christmas leave with their families before going overseas.

It is not surprising that they were bitterly disappointed when the division cancelled all leave over the Christmas period. They soon cheered up when they realised that celebrations were being prepared for them by the local town folk and their officers. In Hemel Hempstead the men of the 17th County of London Battery, 6th London Brigade Royal Field Artillery were treated to an excellent dinner in the Queen Street School. The men had turkey, roast pork, sausages, potatoes and sprouts, followed by plum pudding and bon-bons, apples, nuts and oranges for those who wanted them. There was beer and mineral water and each soldier was given a sixpenny packet of cigarettes. Some of the officers, led by Major Ensor and helped by several ladies, carved the meat, while the non-commissioned officers waited on the men. Some of the officers volunteered for guard duty, so that the men who would otherwise have missed the festivities could join in with their comrades. In the evening it was the turn of the officers to celebrate, and they were treated to an elaborate menu at a large house in Alexandra Road.

On the Wednesday after Christmas the Battery held a concert in the Town Hall with Sergeant Major Annison as master of ceremonies. On New Year's Eve they joined up with other gunners of 5th and 6th Brigades to hold a smoking concert at the Rose and Crown Hotel, in Hemel Hempstead High Street. Sergeant Kemp presided, Corporal Martell played a concertina solo, while Gunner Whiting gave a piano solo, as well as accompanying several vocalists. It was very successful and, perhaps because of the amount of beer consumed, the landlord invited them to hold another concert the following week.

Several of Boxmoor's leading figures contributed to the festivities. Percy Christopherson provided the 12th Battery with an excellent dinner in the gymnasium at Lockers Park School. Some 200 sat down for the dinner, including some men from the Royal Army Medical Corps, and Mr W. Stacey's London Concert Party was invited to come and provide entertainment. The popular novelist Mr William John Locke of Cornerhall, booked Boxmoor Hall and provided the 18th Battery with a Christmas feast and plenty of liquid refreshment and entertainment. Not to be outdone the County Councillor Mitchell Innes put on a dance in Boxmoor Hall for the 18th Battery and the Brigade Headquarters Staff on Boxing Day, and another for the 19th and 20th on the Sunday.

Similar festivities were being carried out elsewhere in West Hertfordshire. In Watford King Edward's Horse celebrated in St. John's Hall, while the 6th City of London Rifles feasted at Boisselier's Cocoa Works and at the Railway Mission Hall. In St Albans units were entertained at Marlborough House, a warehouse in Holywell Hill, The Trumpet, the Clarendon Temperance Hotel in Chequer Street, the County Hall, and the YMCA. in Lattimore Road. A special effort was made to ensure that the wounded soldiers

First World War troops en route through Hertfordshire.

in the Military Hospital at Bricket House had a good Christmas dinner.

If the troops could not have home leave there was nothing to stop the families visiting the area. The Post Office Rifles, some of whom were billeted in Leavesden Mental Hospital, arranged to put on a special show for their families on the evenings of Christmas Day and Boxing Day. The first show went very well. However, at 4 a.m. on Boxing Day the alarm sounded and orders were issued for the men to march from Leavesden to Berkhamsted carrying their full kit. When they arrived at the railway station at Berkhamsted they were ordered to march back again. The six hour march took place in pelting rain and hail on a road so slippery that it was hard to stand up. When they returned to Leavesden the men were tired and stiff,

143

but the show must go on, and after a few hours sleep the planned children's entertainment went ahead.

In addition to the major beanfeasts and concerts a number of officers were invited to spend Christmas with local families. On Christmas Eve Second Lieutenant Pilditch was invited to have dinner with the Lidderdales, of Woodland House, Boxmoor. After drinks, a smoke, and a game of pool he returned to his billet in the Fishery Inn. To keep up the Christmas tradition he forlornly hung up a stocking in which he placed some sweets and a packet of toothpaste. In the morning he was surprised to find that it also contained a box of dates, biscuits, fruit, some fluffy chickens and a small bottle of whisky. The landlord, Edward Hall, clearly wanted to make sure that the officers billeted in his inn had a good Christmas.

A Home Guard troop, 1940.

22 Degrees of Frost

✠

The article, 'Not a Christmas Card Christmas in the grip of the Frost King', appeared in the Welwyn News *on 22 December* 1927.

The cold spell of the end of last week and the beginning of this week provided some unusually low temperatures in Welwyn Garden City. The following readings of glass minima on the Fahrenheit thermometer will be of general interest:

Thursday night	(December 15th)	15 degrees
Friday night	(16th)	13 degrees
Saturday night	(17th)	17 degrees
Sunday night	(18th)	10 degrees
Monday night	(19th)	19 degrees
Tuesday night	(20th)	17 degrees

Thus the lowest reading on Sunday night showed 22 degrees of frost.

The thaw came early on Wednesday morning with a light rain, which, falling upon the frozen roads, was immediately transformed into a glassy surface of ice, and effectually immobilised all wheeled traffic, making even the shortest journey a passage perilous for the pedestrian. The grass verges provided the safest means of progress. Nothing could stand on the roads, and the delivery of the early morning milk was rendered impossible. Buses were suspended. Several tons of grit had been spread on the Urban District roads on

Trees in the snow. Photograph by M. Ashby.

Monday and Tuesday, but for some hours on Wednesday morning the frozen rain on the surface made this ineffective. As horses could not stand it was impossible to get out further sand and shingle for the purpose, but cinders and sawdust were carried and spread as far as practicable. In large numbers of houses the water pipes, which had been frozen for several days, burst with disastrous results, and the demand for the services of plumbers and pipe-fitters was so great that it could not be met.

All householders leaving their houses unoccupied during the Christmas holidays, are warned in case there is a recurrence of frost to take steps to obviate the damage which would result from frost bursts in their absence. The stop-cock should be shut right off and all taps (both hot and cold) turned on full and WCs flushed so as to empty the house pipes completely.

The Joy of Christmas

✛

An article from the Welwyn Garden City and Hertfordshire Pilot *of* 15
December 1922.

Thousands will probably wish themselves dead this Christmas
because they have no work, owing to forces beyond their control.
There are thousands in the hospitals to whom Christmas will bring
no relief from pain and anxiety. Then let us who have health and
work be thankful that we, for some inscrutable reason, are permitted
to spend this Christmas in what must appear the lap of luxury to
men like the one we met today, who had been out of work for two
long weary years. If one did not firmly believe that there is some day
to be an end of pain and suffering, it would be impossible to enjoy
Christmas among the misery that surrounds us.

The story of St George and the Dragon is simply a lovely picture of
how youth, rising in righteous wrath, shall one day overpower those
who oppress the weak and helpless. The lesson of Cinderella, as G.K.
Chesterton says, 'is really the teaching of the Prayer Book that the
humble shall be exalted, because humility is worthy of exaltation...'
Therefore, having done what lies in our power to help the sick and
unemployed, we may 'in peace and tranquillity' for just a few short
days enjoy our England, home and beauty. There is, in our humble
opinion, no more beautiful hymn than 'Christians, Awake, Salute
the Happy Morn', and we wonder how many have remarked and
pondered over the meaning of the concluding words of one verse

147

Father Christmas arriving at Welwyn Stores by helicopter, 1950. Courtesy of the John Lewis Partnership Archive Collection.

Queuing for Father Christmas at Welwyn Stores, *c.* 1945. Courtesy of the John Lewis Partnership Archive Collection.

– 'Till man's first heavenly state takes place'. Poets have an uncanny knack of seeing something which is hidden from the crowd, and we believe the author is here stating a sublime truth which will one day astound the world. We will gladly give the prize of a choice book to the one who in our opinion gives for publication the best explanation of what the author is trying to say in this concluding line.

There is no joy like that of home, and to invite another to enter it is one of the greatest compliments a man can pay to his fellow. If a married man finds no joy in his home it is doubtful whether he will find it elsewhere, and Christmas might be described as the yearly anniversary on which the joys of home should reach their climax. We believe that England will never regain her past glories until the joys of home are what they used to be.

The Shabby Father Christmas
by John Hopkins

From a story first written for the children and teachers of a school in Hoddesdon. Mrs Webber is taking her class to church, and on the way they are observing Christmas displays in the shop windows...

At first, everything went off smoothly, with the children excitedly pointing out robins and holly and other Christmas things in the windows and crossing them off their lists. Then, suddenly, Mrs Webber realised that she was one child short. Quickly she looked round her group. Neil wasn't there.

'Oh, there he is.'

He wasn't far away and was just standing staring at a rather shabby Father Christmas in a shop doorway, who was ringing his bell and calling out to the passing shoppers to persuade them to come in.

Mrs Webber went back a few steps to collect Neil. The Father Christmas was dressed in a thin cotton red robe, his whiskers were rather grubby cotton wool and he wasn't as fat as Father Christmas was supposed to be. Beneath his robe she could see that he wasn't wearing thick fur-topped boots but shoes that were worn and cracked.

'Come along, Neil. We must keep up with the others.'

Neil joined the others as they made their way to the Church, but he was thinking. Thinking about Father Christmas. He wasn't sure about the idea of Father Christmas. He knew the ones in the shops weren't the real Father Christmas. They couldn't be, since one day last week, in Harlow, he'd seen three of them, all in different shops. But the fact that they were dressed like Father Christmas didn't necessarily mean that there wasn't a real one somewhere. After all, in nativity plays, the girls were dressed up as angels with wobbly cardboard wings and white nighties, but that didn't mean that there weren't real angels somewhere.

In the Church the children gathered round the crib, and, when Mrs Webber gave the signal, they began to sing 'Away in a manger'. She liked that carol, she remembered singing it herself when she was a little girl. Behind her, as she conducted the children's singing, the mothers who had helped were sitting in the front pew, gratefully resting their legs. Mrs Webber wished she could sit down too. People didn't realise how tiring teaching could be, for a teacher seldom gets a chance to sit down. She looked at the crib with the baby Jesus and his mother, the cattle kneeling round with the Kings and the shepherds with their gifts. The children sang softly and sweetly. At times like this, she could forget the occasions when they were noisy and fidgety, and when they just would not stop talking, and the times when they could even be downright naughty. At the end of the carol, after the children had admired the crib, she led them back to school where the rest of the mothers would be waiting to take their children home.

The next morning in class, she asked the children to read out their lists and compare results. She told them again the story of the first Christmas, Jesus's Birthday, and the gifts that the Kings and the shepherds had brought.

'Now, children, are there any questions?'

A hand went up at the back. 'Please, Mrs Webber, who gives Father Christmas his presents?'

'I really don't know, why do you ask?' She thought of the shabby old man dressed as Father Christmas that the class had seen in the High Street. He didn't look as if he was likely to get many presents this Christmas.

'Could we all bring some presents and give them to the Father Christmas we saw? It's not fair that he gets left out.'

Mrs Webber thought for a moment. 'I think that is a really generous idea, Peter. If any of you want to bring in a little gift for Father Christmas tomorrow, we will collect them all together and take them to Father Christmas in the High Street. But, remember, you are not to spend too much money. Just bring little things you think he might enjoy.'

The following day the children brought their presents in. A handkerchief from one, some sweets from another. A packet of soup and a bag of crisps. A new biro shaped like a banana. Some of the presents were not suitable but the thought was kind. At the end of school, she took the tallest boy and the tallest girl in the class and, when she had got their mother's permission, she led them down to the High Street with the presents piled in a decorated box. The shabby Father Christmas was still there, ringing his bell and calling out. He did look cold. Mrs Webber was sure that the thin cotton robe did little to keep out the chill wind. When the children gave the presents to Father Christmas he was extremely pleased and blew his nose on a rather ragged handkerchief that he took from his pocket. At least one of the presents would be useful, thought Mrs. Webber.

'Do you think, Ma'am, that I could come to the school tomorrow to say thank you to all the children?'

XMAS CRACKERS AND NOVELTIES

As it is quite impossible to enumerate our enormous and varied stock, we cordially invite you to make an early selection from our Show Room.

BOXES OF CRACKERS, containing a fine assortment of Hats, Caps, Bonnets, Musical Toys, Parlour Fireworks, etc., at prices   from **6d.** to **21/-**

TABLE DECORATIONS.
 We have a large variety at prices ranging from **3/6** to **25/-**

MIDGET CRACKERS	.. per box **6d., 11d., 1/3, 1/6**
CARNIVAL SNOWBALLS (1 dozen) ..	.. per box **1/10** to **3/3**
JOKE BOMBS (Brock's)	.. each **6d., 1/-, 2/6 & 3/6**
NOVELTY CRACKERS (½ dozens) ..	.. per box **5/-** to **7/6**

Paper Costumes, Balloons, Party Hats, etc., etc.

Advertisement for Kingham's Stores, Watford, 1938.

'That's a nice idea, and I am sure the Headmaster won't mind,' answered Mrs Webber, 'but shouldn't you be working here?'

'I'll manage, don't you worry,' said the shabby Father Christmas.

It wasn't till the last lesson of the next day that the Father Christmas knocked on the classroom door and came into the room. He seemed just a little fatter than she remembered, thought Mrs Webber, and surely his robe was made of a rich red velvet and not the

153

thin cotton he had on yesterday. When the Father Christmas spoke, it was in a deep voice with a sort of chuckle in it.

'I wanted to say thank you to you all for the kind presents you sent me yesterday. I know you will all be getting beautiful presents on Christmas Day, so I have brought you a special sort of present, an invisible one. When you thought about bringing me a present, that was a kind thought. When you actually brought the present , that was a kind deed. My present to you is that whenever you have a kind thought, and whenever you do a kind deed, you will feel a warm glow inside you and you will know that that glow is my present to you.' The Father Christmas turned to Mrs Webber.

'A Merry Christmas to you, my dear, and to all the children.' And he kissed her on the cheek. Mrs Webber thought surely the whiskers she felt weren't cotton wool, they were real. With her hands she could feel the rich smoothness of the velvet robe and not the threadbare cotton she had seen yesterday. The Father Christmas turned to leave the classroom and she looked down at his feet. No longer were they wearing thin, cracked shoes, but magnificent fur-topped leather boots. She couldn't understand it, but what was most puzzling of all was, that although it was dry and bright outside, it was not snowing, but there on the toes of Father Christmas's boots was a little heap of snow. As he walked to the door the snow slipped off from the boots and lay melting slowly on the classroom floor. The door closed. Mrs Webber walked quickly to the window. She should be able to see Father Christmas cross the playground to the gate, but although nobody came she was sure that she could hear, ever so faintly, the sound of reindeer bells and a hearty voice calling 'A Happy Christmas to you all'.

A Christmas Past
by Dorothy Cleal

An evocative article about remembered Christmases in east Hertfordshire, first published in the Hertfordshire Countryside *magazine for December 1995. This extract is reprinted here by permission of the author.*

Most of us carry, throughout our lives, an image of at least one childhood Christmas; though, memory being the unreliable record it is, usually several Christmases merge, giving a composite picture, impossible to date.

Christmas for me always conjures up a time in the early 1930s, when home was a cottage in a hamlet on the Herts/Essex border. Times were hard for most of us; my own father was out of work for three years. Yet somehow he and my mother managed to make Christmas a time of real magic for my sister and me. Of course, the old house helped, with its enormous chimney, open to the stars, and the hearth across which my father placed a real Yule log; this burned throughout the two or three days of the Christmas festivities, glowing aromatically, with sparks flying upwards as Dad shifted it across as it burned through. I have a jumbled picture in my mind of the flickering light of candles among dark evergreens, and the glitter of tinsel among the shadows in the corner where the little Christmas tree stood, and the all-pervading scent of logs and orange peel; the memory comes back deliciously as I write.

We loved the build-up to the great event almost more than the festival itself. We started getting the Christmas feeling at Harvest Thanksgiving, along with the smell of apples and paraffin lamps. We welcomed the frosty nip in the air which came soon after. Then Hallowe'en, Bonfire Night, and Advent ('O Come, O come Emmanuel' in the choir and my mother making Christmas puddings and giving us a stir to wish on). Then Christmas cards, often posted nearer the great day than is usual now, I think, but always delivered on time (sometimes on Christmas morning).

They weren't the big, meaningless ritual they have since become; one didn't send to people one saw regularly; each one sent and received was savoured, each a delight. I suppose our family's total each way was about a dozen, and that was probably above average for the hamlet. And we really got our money's worth. As a child I remember only personally sending one card a year, to a little friend in Oxfordshire. She never sent back, because her mother thought cards a waste of money. (Mine cost a ha' penny from Woolworth's, and the stamp was a ha'penny too, if I didn't seal the envelope). My mother sent to her parents, brothers and sisters, and such aunts as remained, to one of whom she always enclosed a shilling, wrapped in cotton wool (and worried in case she was breaking the law, or that someone would steal it).

School broke up quite close to Christmas Eve, and how good it was, that last afternoon!, with no work insisted upon, and the teachers in unnaturally jocular mood (which made us slightly uneasy). We each got an orange and a few improving little booklets and puzzles, issued free by firms like Shredded Wheat ('The Factory in a Garden'). And we giggled a lot, and the boys threw paper pellets without getting told off, while the short December afternoon faded outside and the teachers pulled on the lamps, reminding us uncomfortably (yet

Making the Christmas cake, 1960s. Photograph by M.Ashby.

thrillingly) that it would be dark before we got home.

From the age of about seven I was allowed to go carol-singing with my sister and her friend. We wriggled with excitement as my mother lighted the candle in the triangular lantern, and, well wrapped up, we set out into the darkness. Peggy, the friend, was a giggler; my sister took it very seriously, as I did. We gave real value for money; not for us the old hackneyed ones, 'While Shepherds Watched' and 'Good King Wenceslas'; these were the basic repertoire of the opposition, i.e. the gang from the council houses, who didn't take the business seriously at all, but belted out one verse of each and then thumped on the door; they thought us a cissy bunch, actually enjoying the singing as much as the collecting, and as far as possible we gave them a wide berth. At the end of the evening, during which we had probably covered two or three miles, much of it through dark and sparsely populated lanes, we returned home to scalding cups of cocoa and the excitement of counting the loot. This, as far as I can recall, usually amounted to about half a crown for each of us, mostly in pennies and ha'pennies which, added to our savings (largesse distributed by summer visitors) gave us a nice little sum for buying Christmas presents and other seasonal expenses. Considering the economic climate of the time, I think we did rather well.

Going to Stortford to do our Christmas shopping was a great thrill. One such occasion stands out clearly. It was market day, after school and dark. My father met us there after work, and took charge of me while my mother and sister went off to do their own present buying. He took me to buy fruit from the stalls, which at that time must have carried on their business far into the evening, as did the shops. I found the scene entrancing; all those piles of waxy, gleaming fruit, especially the tangerines, pyramids of orange and silver (fruit, I may say, was something of a luxury in our household); all touched with enchantment in the light from the gas flares, which hissed and flamed fitfully in the chill wind. Then we moved to Woolworth's.

Woolworth's must loom large in the memory of every inter-war child – Woolworth's at any time, for that matter, for it was always magic, and no town was considered a town without that red and gold shop front with the legend 'Nothing over Sixpence' comfortingly emblazoned. We never thought the day would come when dear old Woollies would close in High Street after High Street. In the 1930s, it seemed that it would go on for ever, part of the urban scenery, like fish and chip shops, the Co-op and the Home and Colonial. To say that a child entering Woolworth's in that era was like entering Aladdin's Cave may be trite but it was the very truth. Who can forget the smell, and the brown floorboards which, though bare, had a curious softness? My first impression in my tender years was a forest of legs; at just about eye level were the counters, when one could get to them, and what a feast they were at that time of year! I loved the counter offering Christmas tree baubles, tinsel, and paper chains, looped up to the ceiling, a riot of colour and glitter; and it was here that I saw for the first time Christmas wrapping paper; until then, presents had just come brown-wrapped; this new paper had a design of holly – there were no others – and the notice said: 'Make Your Gifts Look Christmassy!' – a novel idea; but it was many years before it was used in our family, being considered an unnecessary extravagance ('What will they think of next to part you from your money!' my mother said).

Our purchases made, we came out into the cold and crowded street, and it was then that I had the only uneasy moment of that memorable evening. The occasion was the sight of a poor old man (perhaps an old soldier?) pathetically dragging himself along in a travesty of Father Christmas robes, all hunched up against the cold, trying unsuccessfully to sell tawdry little toys from a tray. I didn't question my father, but wrestled with my confusion and sadness in private, but the image haunted me, and is with me still.

The Grand Duke Michael's Knebworth Christmas

✠

The full story can be read in Michael and Natasha *by Rosemary and Donald Crawford, published by Weidenfeld & Nicolson, 1997.*

In 1912, the Grand Duke Michael, brother of Tsar Nicholas II of

The servants' hall at Knebworth House, 1 January 1914.

Russia, made a runaway marriage to the beautiful, but divorced, Natasha. Exiled from Russia, they came to England and in 1913 rented Knebworth House from the Earl of Lytton. Here they enjoyed a year of tranquillity before the First World War broke out and they returned to Russia, to face war, revolution and ultimate tragedy.

The Christmas Michael and Natasha spent at Knebworth was a happy one, with celebrations in both the English and the Russian traditions. The English on 25 December 1913 and the Russian on 6 January 1913. They combined the two worlds on 1 January 1913 by giving a magnificent dinner and ball for the servants.

Menu card for the servants' ball at Knebworth. The signatures on the back include that of the Grand Duke Michael.

A Family Christmas
at Borehamwood

by Christine Hardman

Currently Archdeacon of Lewisham, the Revd Christine Hardman was previously curate at the church of St John the Baptist, Markyate then vicar of Holy Trinity, Stevenage. She and her husband, Roger, grew up in Borehamwood.

Before I was born Borehamwood must have been a little village clustered round its High Street. Then, after the Second World War, there was an enormous amount of building by the London County Council (LCC) to provide what were called 'overspill' estates for Londoners who had been bombed out or otherwise made homeless. Our estate – Manor Way estate – was one of the oldest.

My father was a teacher in Fulham and he was allocated an LLC house in Borehamwood. He travelled to work by bus every day – a dreadful journey. I was a year old when we moved in 1952 into our brand new house. My mother said it was surrounded by a sea of mud. All these new estates were about one to two miles from the centre of Borehamwood, and people always talked of 'going down to the village', to the Shenley Road shops.

We did not have a car, so there were the logistics of my mother and father going shopping together for the Christmas food. This was not done until a day or so before Christmas, as we had no refrigerator and meat was stored in a meat safe in the larder. By this time, I remember, there was a bus service. My parents had to carry all the shopping in heavy bags by bus and one of my earliest memories is of my father staggering home absolutely laden with shopping bags.

The shop I remember most vividly was the old Sainsbury's, before the days of supermarkets, on the left as you went towards Elstree station. It did not have a very wide frontage, but it went back a long way and was tiled in green and white. Inside there were very long counters, where you queued at different points for different food – this was before the days of self-service. We moved from queue to queue inside the shop. I was very impressed by the lady staff who all had their hair in white nets. My father liked this shop because he was passionate about bacon and he thought Sainsbury's bacon was good, so we always did our Christmas food shopping here. We never had a turkey, but always a capon, at Christmas.

Christmas trees were on sale outside the greengrocer's. I remember my father coming home with a small one. But at that time Christmas did not start until a day or two before Christmas Eve. At primary school we always had some kind of nativity play, or a Christmas play. One year it was Cinderella. I was usually given a part, then got bronchitis and ended up not doing it. At the end of every term I always got bronchitis, which went on for two weeks or so, with the doctor calling every day at first.

We had a class Christmas party at school. The teacher made a list of what we could bring and our mothers sent jellies, cakes and biscuits. We played traditional games such as musical chairs, statues, squeak-piggy-squeak. The girls dressed up in their party dresses and it was tremendously exciting, although there were no prizes and no take-home bags. The school was built in the early 1950s. It was the time of the post-war bulge and there were two classes for every year group, with forty-five children in each. One teacher, with no help, took each class.

Christmas decorations were quite a big thing for us. At home my mother, my sister and I made yards and yards of paper chains. One year we thought we were very stylish, with red and white crêpe paper chains folded over and over. We festooned the room with them and also the tissue-paper bells that opened out.

My first memory of our Christmas tree was of lighted candles, but these were not used again for safety reasons. Thereafter we had an annual drama with chunky coloured lights. For some reason they never had a plug of their own and my father always took the plug off some other appliance and returned it after Christmas. The lights never worked first time and there was no fuse bulb, so we had to check each light individually.

One year, in the mid-1950s, we had a television in time for Christmas. It was a Pye, with a very small screen. We bought a clip-on contrivance, made of curved, transparent glass or plastic and filled with an inflammable liquid, which was supposed to magnify the picture. Many people had them, but their popularity was short-lived, as they were the cause of some terrible fires.

My grandparents lived only two miles away, but they always came to stay for Christmas. When they arrived on Christmas Eve I knew it had really begun. My grandmother would bring a small plastic doll, beautifully dressed in silver and white crêpe paper, for the Christmas tree fairy. My sister and I took it in turns to keep it each year. We also had an enormous ritual about Father Christmas. We left him a glass of sherry, a mince pie and a cigarette – and some crusts for the reindeer, before we went to bed. One year my father had made me

Members of the Hardman family celebrate Christmas Day, *c.* 1960. Photograph by John Hardman.

a doll's house and he and my mother and grandparents worked until two o'clock in the morning to finish it.

There was a postal delivery on Christmas Day and we always had a big parcel from my father's brothers and sisters in Wales. They had a Post Office and shop in a small village and were always too busy to attend to Christmas presents until the last minute. Then they took a cardboard box and filled it with things from their own stock; Bunty Annuals, selections of sweets and any other odd thing that they thought we might like. It was like an Aladdin's treasure trove, a whole collection of surprises.

On Christmas morning we enlisted my grandmother's help so that we could get up early. She would go down and make tea, then we could wake everyone and open our presents before breakfast. We usually had one main present and fruit, nuts and sweets in our stockings. The Christmas Day lunch was looked forward to as a very important family occasion and celebration. We ate food we did not usually have, including bread sauce to a special recipe and Christmas pudding with sixpences inside. Afterwards there were crackers and Grandfather smoked his pipe.

Boxing Day was much lower key, a very relaxed time, with my grandparents still there, watching us play with our toys. The next day things returned to normal. The whole Christmas period was very short. I cannot remember when the decorations were taken down, but I know they did not last for twelve days.

For me, as a child, Christmas Day had enormous significance, a tremendous sense of magic. The ordinary was, for a couple of days, transformed. The living room became something magical, with the colours, the decorations, the lights in the tree. There was the almost-too-painful-to-bear anticipation – what would Father Christmas bring? In the darkness of winter this was a very special time.

Hospital Christmas Memories
by Enid King

Enid King (née Pedley) did her SRN training with St Bartholomew's Hospital during the Second World War, during which time it was transferred to Hill End, near St Albans. She later worked at Hitchin, first as a midwife, then as a health visitor. A car accident in 1960 left her paralysed from the waist down. In 1972 she wrote Rushed Off My Feet, *which was published by Heinemann.*

At the outbreak of the Second World War in 1939, Hill End Hospital, designed to accommodate mentally ill patients, was taken over by St Bartholomew's Hospital, London EC1, and used as a general hospital, transferring air raid casualties and emergency cases from London as soon as they could be moved to the safety of the countryside. The Medical School and the School of Nursing were also transferred from London to Hill End.

Every effort was made to celebrate Christmas in a traditional way. Decorations were put up on Christmas Eve and made from any materials that were available. Cotton wool snow flakes abounded on the windows and the glass panels of the doors. Holly and ivy entwined the door frames and mistletoe hung from the ceiling lamps. Sprigs of mistletoe were also hidden under the party hats worn by the patients, to be used on any unsuspecting Nurse who came near enough. On the evening of Christmas Eve, carols were sung. The medical students, carrying lanterns fixed on long poles, and the nurses, with their capes turned to show the red lining and carrying torches, sung as they walked in slow procession round every ward.

None of the nursing staff had leave on Christmas Day. All essential nursing duties were carried out and, by tradition, it was the Sister and Staff Nurse who did the bedpan round. The turkey was carved by the houseman. Entertainment was provided by the Medical Students who formed themselves into several groups, going from ward to ward, performing cabaret acts, pantomimes and community singing. The Hospital Chaplain gave Holy Communion by the bedside of all the patients who wished it and church services were held in the Hospital Chapel at times convenient for day and night nursing staff.

Although separated from their loved ones at home, Christmas in hospital can be one of the happiest memories for both Staff and patients.

Footnote: Unexpected drama occurred when a nurse swallowed a pin while fixing the ward decorations. The Emergency Operating Team, on standby over Christmas, were alerted as it was feared that 'perforation of the gut' might occur. Enquiries as to the progress of the pin were numerous but, in due time, the cotton wool sandwiches proved their worth and the pin passed in the usual manner. The whispered 'congratulations' to the nurse from staff and patients alike did nothing to spare her blushes.

The Infant Welfare Clinic mothers and babies party at Hitchin Town Hall, Christmas 1954. Dr Vernon Walker, Medical Officer of Health for North Herts, is in the front row, dressed as Father Christmas. He is holding Richard, aged eight months, the son of Health Visitor Enid Pedley, who is far right, with a handbag on her arm. Courtesy of Home Counties Newspapers.

St Nicholas of Myra
– the Real Santa Claus
by Don Dowling

There are seven churches in Hertfordshire dedicated to St Nicholas. These are at Elstree, Great Hormead, Great Munden, Harpenden, Hinxworth, Norton and Stevenage. The Revd Don Dowling, vicar of St Nicholas', Stevenage explains how the saint became known as Father Christmas.

St Nicholas whose feast day is celebrated on 6th December was a fourth-century Bishop of Myra in Asia Minor – Lycia in modern Turkey. We cannot be sure of his actual dates, but the traditional date of his death is 6th December 343. He is reputed to have suffered imprisonment during the Emperor Diocletian's persecution in 303-304 and attended the great council of Nicea, which sought to settle some major issues of orthodox Christian doctrine. However, we have no record of this.

What is perhaps more interesting to us are the stories which developed around him shortly after his death making him one of the most popular Christian saints. The fact that he is the patron saint of merchants, bankers, pawnbrokers, children, sailors and of Russia, as well as of many medieval churches, witnesses to the breadth of his popularity. There are more than 400 churches dedicated to him in Britain, of which seven are in Hertfordshire.

The early legends

An early story about bishop Nicholas lies at the heart of today's Santa Claus. One version, and there are several, goes like this. There was a merchant in Patara who had lost all his money. He had three daughters to support who could not find husbands because of their poverty; so the wretched man was going to sell them into prostitution. This came to the ears of Nicholas, who thereupon took a bag of gold and, under cover of darkness threw it in through the open window of the man's house. Here was a dowry for the eldest girl and she was soon duly married. Later Nicholas repeated this action for the second and third daughters; on the last night this happened the father was watching out. Recognizing his benefactor he overwhelmed him with his gratitude. Incidentally, the purses are supposed to have landed in stockings hanging by the fire, which marks the origin of the custom of putting up stockings by the chimney for gifts from St Nicholas.

The three purses represented in pictures, in time came to be mistaken for the heads of three children. This gave rise to the far-fetched story of three boys, who had been killed by an innkeeper and pickled in a brine-tub. St Nicholas miraculously raised them to life. You may have seen the tale depicted on stained-glass windows. This legend is responsible for his being honoured as the patron saint of barrel makers. Interestingly enough, these same three purses, or bags of gold, became the three golden balls of the familiar sign for pawnbrokers.

Patron saint of sailors

St Nicholas is also the patron saint of sailors. Hence one of his symbols is that of a ship. The story goes that during his lifetime, the saint appeared to mariners in peril from a terrible storm off the Lycian coast. They had invoked his aid, and he brought them safely to their harbour. Following a common Eastern custom, sailors in the Eastern Mediterranean named a certain star 'the star of St Nicholas' when it rose in the skies. They also wished one another a good voyage in the phrase 'May St Nicholas hold the tiller'. In the eleventh century, when his homeland was under threat, sailors from Bari spirited away his relics then placed them in a shrine of the Basilica di San Nicola where they remain to this day. This act was not purely disinterested since in the middle ages there was a lot of money to be made if your town had custody of the bones of a famous saint.

The transformation

So how did the transformation of the fourth-century bishop of Myra into Santa Claus come about? We owe this to the Dutch. In the Netherlands St Nicholas was known as Sinta Klaas. Over the course of time a whole series of tales were woven around him. In popular culture Sinta Klaas arrived by steamship from Spain on his white horse accompanied by grim servant Black Peter (the devil). Dutch children put out hay or carrots in their shoes for the horse to encourage gifts from Sinta Klaas! When St Nicholas arrived he would instruct his servant to give the good children rewards, sometimes consulting a large book where the children's behaviour was noted. Those who had been naughty were birched, or spirited away by Black Peter.

Dutch settlers in America continued these customs in New Amsterdam (New York). Eventually, with a good push from

Santa Claus with presents for good children; an Edwardian Christmas image.

commercial interests, they become fused with the Nordic figure of Father Christmas and his reindeer, and the custom of giving presents to mark Christmas.

The descriptions of St Nicholas in the writings of the American author Washington Irving and, slightly later, in a very popular poem by Clement Clark Moore, which he wrote for his children, mark the beginning of this transformation. For instance in Moore's poem, 'A Visit from St Nicholas', (usually known as The Night before Christmas), Santa is imagined as a fat jolly elf clothed in fur and stained with soot. (Probably as a result of descending from chimneys!) The final twist in this transformation of Santa Klaus was given a huge boost by Coca Cola in its 1920s Christmas Santa advertising campaign, in which the colour of Santa's coat was changed from the traditional green to red.

There is a fascinating website www.stnicholascenter.org *containing lots of information about St Nicholas and Christmas customs.*

Letters from the Boer War
by Sue Fisher

Sue Fisher, journalist and deputy editor of the Comet *newspaper, researched the archives of its predecessor, the* Hertfordshire Express, *to produce her book* Lust, Dust and Cobblestones, *which she describes as a 'personal look' at Hitchin and the surrounding area between 1900 and 1913. The following extracts are reprinted here with her permission.*

Private S. Brown wrote to his mother in Dunstable, describing his Christmas Day:

We have only coffee and bread to eat and my only comfort was my good old pipe. As we lay in the trenches the bullets came over us like hail storm and the shrieks of the shells sounded like the wind in the telegraph wires on a rough night.

The heat during the daytime is unbearable and as we lay in the trenches and looked towards the hills from where the Boers were firing I thought that if mother could see me now she would hardly enjoy her Christmas.

But we enjoyed ourselves as well as we could in the circumstances.

On Christmas Day we lay in the trenches and sang songs, one of the favourite songs being 'A soldier and a man whatever my fate'. May I be a soldier and a man.

[...] I am not in the best of health; I think it is through drinking the dirty water from the [River] Modder and the hot country. The dust gets down our throats and makes us drink heavily of the river water. And then we are short of food. If I live to come home the first thing I will enjoy is a good feed and I can tell you I am looking forward to it.

Gunner William Silsby of Hitchin wrote of fighting in the heat of battle:
We have lost all our officers who were all shot down and also our sergeant major was shot right through the head. It was an awful sight; I shall never forget it as long as I live...

I was standing at my gun, the bullets falling all around me. I was loading as quickly as I could and my fingers were bleeding with pulling out the pins. The sun was burning hot, my neck was skinned with the sun and my water bottle and haversack skinned my neck too and my number one was shot and lying at my feet. The poor fellows were shot and falling all over the place and at this time our ammo had expired. I had just loaded the last shell I had left and then we had an order to leave.

I don't know what sort of Christmas you had at home but I do not want another like ours. I had just a drink of water out of my bottle which had been in for two days. Our Christmas dinner was a bit of fat which we had to throw away. I wish I was a good reader and writer, I would show up those who have put in the papers that we get good and plenty.

Christmas Day in the Hitchin Union Workhouse

by Sue Fisher

Another extract from Lust, Dust and Cobblestones.

Christmas was a special time even at the workhouse and the holiday in 1903 was 'one of the happiest days they had spent in the institution,' reported the *Express*.

The 192 inmates were given additional food to eat, starting with extra sweet strong tea at breakfast. For lunch they tucked into roast pork, parsnips and plum pudding while the patients in the infirmary could have rabbit if they preferred.

Every man was given tobacco and a pint of beer or, if teetotal, mineral water, while the women had extra tea with sugar. Oranges were distributed to everybody.

Tea included half a pound of cake each, followed by entertainment as matron kindly played the piano for the older inmates, who apparently retired to bed well pleased. Prominent families in the town sent evergreens for decorations and supplied toys and oranges. Some took their philanthropy very seriously and called in to see the inmates in person during the afternoon.

[...] During Christmas 1908 there were 224 people in Hitchin workhouse. 'One little privilege that was greatly appreciated was when the old people in the infirmary of both sexes were allowed to dine together, a thing they had never done before,' reported the *Express*.

The children who were given their presents from the tree on New Year's Eve were taken to a pantomime in the town and, at Hitchin Hospital, Santa brought five bundles of clothes on Christmas Eve along with toys for the children.

The girls from Scott House invited 30 workhouse children to tea. Their table looked very pretty, laden with cakes, fruit and crackers. After tea at 4 p.m. the children enjoyed a play, games and music, singing and dancing. Every girl was given a doll nicely dressed with garments to take on and off, while the boys went back with trumpets. 'One little fellow asked if he might take a cracker home for his brother so a parcel was made of things left over from the tea and given him to take back to those who were prevented from coming.'

Christmas in German prisoner-of-war camp, 1940

The Revd John King as a German prisoner of war.

Christmas as a Prisoner of War

by John King

✝

The Revd John Humphrey King was born at St Albans in 1908, educated at Berkhamsted, then as a choral scholar at King's College, Cambridge, where he graduated with a degree in Classics. He became a priest in 1934. During the Second World War he served in the Royal Army Chaplain's Department and for five years, between June 1940 and April 1945, he was a prisoner of the Germans. After his release, he became successively rector of Stevenage, rural dean of Hitchin, rector of St Paul's, Bedford and finally returned to St Albans as honorary canon of the diocese. Throughout all the dangers, hardships and restrictions, he managed to write up his diary and this remarkable and inspiring journal has now been published by his family with the title Thank you, Padre.

Sunday 22 December 1940

'Der Tag!' Up at 6.30am for a 7.00am Mass in the hospital. But just after I had woken up the intending communicants, and was rigging my altar, all the lights in the block went out. The air-raid warning of 1.00am had been repeated. I searched for candles or night lights in vain, then knelt at the table in the middle of the silent inky ward hoping to have lights on again at any moment. But after forty minutes all was still in darkness, and I had to pack up and creep away lest the G[erman] orderlies should arrive and find me there. We are not supposed to say Mass there; though we do it catacomb wise every Sunday.

[...] At 12.30 I held a final run-through of the Carol Service in the theatre; choir, orchestra and readers. The orchestra's entries were deplorable; so bad that even they were shocked – which cheered me, as it meant they would be on tip-toe in the evening. They were.

From 2.30-4.00pm I went to bed and tried deliberately to sleep; but was much too excited and on edge. So I lay and read 'Pip' the most soothing book in the room! After tea, the final preparations. David Wild and Major West had decorated the tree, and I had arranged the altar in front of it; with silvered cross, and six tall candles 2" thick in candlesticks which were lovely slim hock bottles with grease catchers. Then up to the gallery at the back of the room. At 5.55pm I brought them in; then signalled 'all set' to David who was at the far end of the room downstairs. He saw that everybody was seated, then winked at Saunders to stop him; then got the packed congregation to its feet. Then, almost like King's: 'Once in Royal David's City' came out of the gallery, without warning, solo tenor, unaccompanied. Verse by verse other voices joined in, then the orchestra and for the last two verses the 400 men below.

So began Laufen's first Carol Service. Following the King's tradition it went on, slowly unfolding the Incarnation. Even in my secret heart I had not dared to hope it would be so beautiful. Downstairs, as I looked over the gallery edge, I saw the room packed with men, of every rank from Brigadier to Private. They faced an altar, white-dressed with its silvered cross and six tall candles. Behind it in the alcove towered the great tree, white with 200 frosty balls and 50 white candles. Above hung a pendant light turned into a star.

Nine readers, one of every rank, were near the lectern. Upstairs I had my coat and jersey off, and stood on my conductor's tub wet with sweat, and nearly intoxicated with excitement. I had always been shy of conducting – till tonight. They say I did better than usual. I know that I was standing on the tips of my toes. Both singers and players excelled themselves; never so well before. So the service swept smoothly and inexorably toward the Christmas gospel. During 'While Shepherds watched' all the candles on the tree were lighted one by one, and all the house lights were put out. I caught sight of this over my shoulder and it nearly did for me.

On and on, and finally 'Hark the Herald Angels': singers, orchestra, brass, congregation full throated. From the moment it was over I was absolutely whacked. But people ever since have been stopping me all day long. 'The most wonderful service I've ever been to', 'Why don't we have them at home?' 'We ought to have broadcast', 'It was worth being a prisoner to have heard that.' The last remark came from a wee man from Gateshead and he meant it. It has made me terribly happy. At last a Padre has been of manifest use in Laufen.

Copies of Thank You Padre *are available from Margaret Millard, Trotters, 4 Gransden Road, Caxton, Cambridge, CB3 8PL, at £12.75 plus £3 p&p. Cheques payable to M. Millard.*

Tom Tiddler's Ground
by Charles Dickens

In the summer of 1861, Charles Dickens paid a visit to his friend Edward Bulwer Lytton at Knebworth House. While staying there, he went to see James Lucas, the famous and tragic 'Hermit' who lived in squalor in his decaying family home at Redcoats Green, between Stevenage and Hitchin. The meeting prompted Dickens to write 'Tom Tiddler's Ground', which was published as his Christmas Story for 1861 and subsequently included in the collected edition, Christmas Stories from Household Words and All the Year Round *by Charles Dickens, published by J.M. Dent in their Everyman series in 1910.*

'And why Tom Tiddler's ground?' asked the Traveller.

'Because he scatters halfpence to tramps and such-like,' returned the Landlord, 'and of course they pick 'em up. And this being done on his own land (which it *is* his own land, you observe, and were his family's before him), why it is but regarding the halfpence as gold and silver, and turning the ownership of the property a bit round your finger, and there you have the name of the children's game complete. And it's appropriate too,' said the Landlord, with his favourite action of stooping a little, to look across the table out of the window at a vacancy, under the window-blind which was half drawn down. 'Leastwise it has been so considered by many gentlemen which have partook of chops and tea in the present humble parlour.'

The Traveller was partaking of chops and tea in the present humble parlour, and the Landlord's shot was fired obliquely at him.

'And you call him a Hermit?' said the Traveller.

'They call him such,' returned the Landlord, evading personal responsibility; 'he is in general so considered.'

'What *is* a Hermit?' asked the traveller.

'What is it?' repeated the Landlord, drawing his hand across his chin.

'Yes, what is it?'

The Landlord stooped again, to get a more comprehensive view of vacancy under the window-blind, and – with an asphyxiated appearance on him as one unaccustomed to definition – made no answer.

'I'll tell you what I suppose it to be,' said the Traveller. 'An abominable dirty thing.'

'Mr Mopes is dirty, it cannot be denied,' said the Landlord.

'Intolerably conceited.'

'Mr Mopes is vain of the life he leads, some do say,' replied the Landlord, as another concession.

'A slothful, unsavoury, nasty reversal of the laws of human nature,' said the traveller; 'and for the sake of God's working world and its wholesomeness, both moral and physical, I would put the thing on the treadmill (if I had my way) wherever I found it; whether on a pillar, or in a hole; whether on Tom Tiddler's ground, or the Pope of Rome's ground, or a Hindoo fakeer's ground, or any other ground.'

'I don't know about putting Mr Mopes on the treadmill,' said the Landlord, shaking his head very seriously. 'There ain't a doubt but what he has got landed property.'

'How far may it be to this said Tom Tiddler's ground?' asked the Traveller.

'Put it at five mile,' returned the Landlord.

'Well! When I have done my breakfast,' said the Traveller, 'I'll go there. I came over this morning, to find it out and see it.'

'Many does,' observed the Landlord.

Mr Traveller, having finished his breakfast and paid his moderate score, walked out to the threshold of the Peal of Bells, and, thence directed by the pointing finger of his host, betook himself towards the ruined hermitage of Mr Mopes the hermit.

For, Mr Mopes, by suffering everything about him to go to ruin, and by dressing himself in a blanket and skewer, and by steeping himself in soot and grease and other nastiness, had acquired great renown in all that countryside – far greater renown than he could ever have won for himself, if his career had been that of any ordinary Christian, or decent Hottentot. He had even blanketed and skewered and greased himself into the London papers. And it was curious to find, as Mr Traveller found by stopping for a new direction at this farmhouse or that cottage as he went along, with how much accuracy the morbid Mopes had counted on the weakness of his neighbours to embellish him. A mist of home-brewed marvel and romance surrounded Mopes, in which (as in all fogs) the real proportions of the real object were extravagantly heightened. He had murdered his beloved in a fit of jealousy and was doing penance; he had made a vow under the influence of grief; he had made a vow under the influence of a fatal accident; he had made a vow under the influence of religion; he had made a vow under the influence of drink; he had made a vow under the influence of disappointment; he had never made any vow, but 'had got led into it' by the possession of a mighty and most awful secret; he was enormously rich, he was

A snow scene near Weston, 2004. Photograph by Peter Jones.

stupendously charitable, he was profoundly learned, he saw spectres, he knew and could do all kinds of wonders. Some said he went out every night, and was met by terrified wayfarers stalking along dark roads, others said he never went out, some knew his penance to be nearly expired, others had positive information that his seclusion was not a penance at all, and would never expire but with himself. Even, as to the easy facts of how old he was, or how long he had held verminous occupation of his blanket and skewer, no consistent information was to be got, from those who must know if they would. He was represented as being all the ages between five-and-twenty and sixty, and as having been a hermit seven years, twelve, twenty, thirty, – though twenty, on the whole, appeared the favourite term.

'Deep and crisp and even.' Photograph by M. Ashby.

'Well, well!' said Mr Traveller. 'At any rate, let us see what a real live Hermit looks like.'

So, Mr Traveller went on, and on, and on, until he came to Tom Tiddler's ground.

Christmas at Longbourn

by Jane Austen

✠

Pride and Prejudice enthusiasts in Hertfordshire have long debated the exact whereabouts of Longbourn, which Jane Austen has unequivocally located in our county. Her statement that 'The village of Longbourn was only one mile from Meryton', taken in conjunction with other evidence, has given rise to the suggestion that Hertingfordbury was the inspiration for Longbourn and Hertford for Meryton. The following extracts describe the Bennet family's Hertfordshire Christmas.

On the following Monday, Mrs Bennet had the pleasure of receiving her brother and his wife, who came as usual to spend the Christmas at Longbourn. Mr Gardiner was a sensible, gentlemanlike man, greatly superior to his sister as well by nature as education. The Netherfield ladies would have had difficulty in believing that a man who lived by trade, and within view of his own warehouses, could have been so well bred and agreeable. Mrs Gardiner, who was several years younger than Mrs Bennett and Mrs Philips, was an amiable, intelligent, elegant woman, and a great favourite with all her Longbourn nieces. Between the two eldest and herself especially, there subsisted a very particular regard. They had frequently been staying with her in town.

The first part of Mrs Gardiner's business on her arrival was to distribute her presents and describe the newest fashions. When this was done, she had a less active part to play. It became her turn to listen. Mrs Bennet had many grievances to relate, and much to complain of. They had all been very ill-used since she last saw her sister. Two of her girls had been on the point of marriage, and after all there was nothing in it.

The Gardiners staid a week at Longbourn; and what with the Philipses, the Lucases, and the officers, there was not a day without its engagement. Mrs Bennet had so carefully provided for the entertainment of her brother and sister that they did not once sit down to a family dinner. When the engagement was for home, some of the officers always made part of it, of which officers Mr Wickham was sure to be one; and on these occasions, Mrs Gardiner, rendered suspicious by Elizabeth's warm commendation of him, narrowly observed them both. Without supposing them, from what she saw, to be very seriously in love, their preference for each other was plain enough to make her a little uneasy; and she resolved to speak to Elizabeth on the subject before she left Hertfordshire, and represent to her the imprudence of encouraging such an attachment.

Cold Christmas

✠

Tucked away off the A10 road through east Hertfordshire is a cluster
of dwellings surrounded by wide, arable fields. It could easily be passed
unnoticed, except for its name...

In the village of Thundridge, a few miles north of Ware, is the hamlet
of Cold Christmas. Its intriguing name was researched by William
A. Bagley, whose article, 'Round and about Cold Christmas', was
published in the winter issue of the *Hertfordshire Countryside* magazine
for 1965. The earliest document he discovered in the Hertfordshire
Archives was a conveyance dated 1557 which referred to a house and
adjoining land called 'Lyndseys alias Chrystemas' which implies that
this was Lyndsey's property.

Other documents dating from 1729 refer to 'Linseys alias Christens
and now ... [called] Cold Christmas'. Bagley speculated that
'Christmas' may be a personal name and said that he had found over
thirty people in the London telephone directory with the surname
Christmas. He further suggested that the name may have originated
with people born on Christmas Day.

As for 'Cold', Bagley pointed out that this is a very common
element in place-names and that it sometimes signifies an exposed
location, although it he did not think that applied to the Hertfordshire
Cold Christmas, in the valley of the River Rib. He suggested that
'it could also signify cold in the sense that a gardener uses the term.
Cold soil (waterlogged clay for example) is that through which

the warm rays of the sun penetrate slowly, and many of our well-farmed Hertfordshire fields of today were originally undrained and waterlogged – 'cold' in fact.

The hamlet of Cold Christmas, near Thundridge. Photograph by M. Ashby.

Carol singing, 1884.